Printed in the United States of America

Spirit Media and our logos are trademarks of
Spirit Media

SpiritMedia.US

www.spiritmedia.us
8045 Arco Corporate Dr STE 130
Raleigh, NC 27617
1 (888) 800-3744

Books › Christian Books & Bibles › Christian Living ›
Spiritual Growth

Paperback ISBN: 979-8-89307-049-1
Hardback ISBN: 979-8-89307-051-4
Audiobook ISBN: 979-8-89307-052-1
eBook ISBN: 979-8-89307-050-7
Library of Congress Control Number: 2024909819

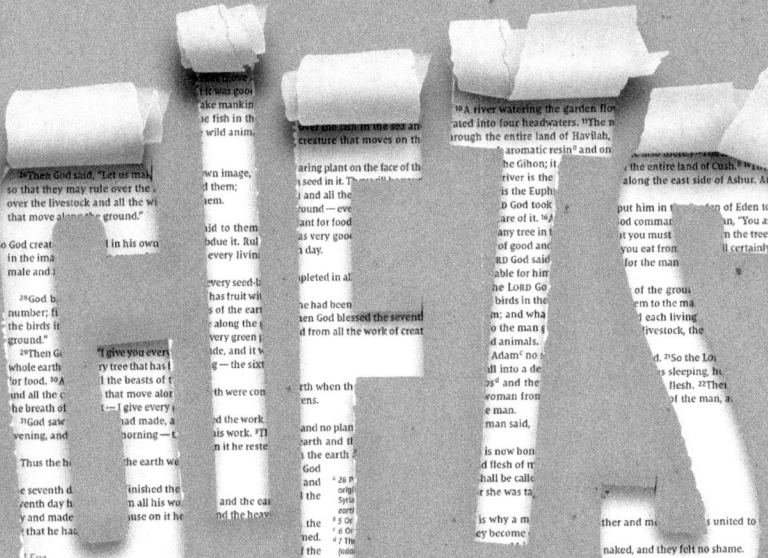

GIFTS

Everything God Promises to Give You in the Bible

KEVIN WHITE

GIFTS

Everything God Promises to Give You in the Bible

Kevin White

2024 © by Kevin White

BIBLE SCRIPTURES

This book would not be possible without the support of:

Glory Suresh and Ana Marie Banares, thank you for helping me to carefully research and collect every reference of God's GIFTS found in the Bible.

Lori Loomis, thank you for helping me edit and glue this book together.

My beautiful team and family at Spirit Media, thank you to everyone who researched keywords, proofread, designed the cover, interior layout, and handled the publishing on Amazon and every where books are sold.

To my Heavenly Father, from whom all blessings flow, to you be the glory for each and every GIFT.

"What do you have that God hasn't GIVEN you? And if everything you have is from God, why boast as though it were not a GIFT?"

–1 Corinthians 4:7 (NLT)

TABLE OF CONTENTS

INTRODUCTION

THE FATHER'S GOING TO GIVE IT!

My fifth book, *Only God Works: Investing Now What Matters Then,* ends with a one sentence conclusion:

Conclusion

The Father's going to give it!
Only God works.

As soon as I finished writing that book, I sensed God's instructions to leave Spirit Media in His hands and go to India and Nepal to teach this revelation.

Spirit Media wasn't even one year old. We'd been struggling to secure enough funding to keep the company going. Our rapid growth had exceeded our available cash flow. We were living month-to-month, wondering if we'd be able to pay our bills and make it to the next month. We had no choice but to depend on the GIFTS of God daily for our very survival. (DEPEND is the final chapter of this book for a reason. More on that later.)

We were confident every investor, staff, client, and project was a GIFT from God. In the middle of all this God tested me to see if I would depend on my human efforts or on His GIFTS. Earlier in my life I had failed this test. This time, I knew better. "I said, 'Yes, Lord'", and prepared to leave this startup company for two weeks for an international mission trip.

Our team at Spirit Media published Only God Works in 14 days! I set out for my fifty-fourth trip to India in twenty-five years and my first ever trip to Nepal. I had been asked to speak multiple times a day high in the hills of Northeast India and Nepal. We gave out copies of Only God Works as God had me proclaim 1 Thessalonians 5:24 (NLT), "God will make this happen, for he who calls you is faithful."

I spent one week in India and a second week in Nepal. It was a fast-paced, life-changing experience. I grew in the Lord; God worked in and through me in a mighty way for His glory, and Spirit Media experienced measurable growth even while I was gone for two weeks. The only possible explanation is: The Father promised to GIVE it and He did!

Everywhere I turned, I saw the GIFTS of God. I'm convinced God took me to India and Nepal to intentionally show me hundreds of millions of dollars of human need. Leaders in India and Nepal were constantly asking me to pray for God's guidance and provision over insurmountable human needs.

We asked God for miraculous physical healings, land, buildings, church facilities, retreat centers, leadership training facilities, salaries for pastors, transportation for pastors, as well as food for the poor, widows, and lepers. We asked God for education for children, homes for orphans, Bible colleges, seminaries, salaries for faculty, libraries, dorms, auditoriums, water projects, baptistries, books, Bibles, marriages, jobs, income generation projects, and more. Truly, the list was endless.

Any human soul would be totally crushed and devastated if it weren't for the revelation: The Father's going to GIVE it!

Because of this revelation we were free to pray with such boldness and confidence knowing: The Father's going to GIVE it! This revelation is absolutely a total game changer! It doesn't matter how big the bill or problem: The GIVER is going to GIVE it or we were not meant to have it.

I'm convinced God took me over 8,000 miles away to India and Nepal to rub my nose in all He desires to GIVE. We literally prayed over hundreds of millions of dollars of human need and Kingdom good.

Before going to India, I was consumed in leading Spirit Media to generate its first million in revenue. I specifically remember, while in India, God telling me: "You're thinking too small." This totally changed my perspective that day. It continues! Multiple times since then, God regularly confronts me with: "You're thinking too small."

We must first accept the revelation that the Father's going to GIVE it. God forbid it takes you as long as it took me to understand this. Once we do, we begin to understand: either The GIVER will GIVE it, or we will never have it. We see our Heavenly Father as The GIVER. We understand that everything we have has been GIVEN to us from Him. We can take no credit for it. As soon as we agree with Him that the Father's going to GIVE it, He begins to show us just how much He desires to GIVE to us.

For two solid weeks in India and Nepal, God kept showing me things He would love to GIVE: GIFTS that would bless His people, extend His kingdom, accomplish His mission, and bring Him glory. With each exposure to human need, I sensed God asking: would you be willing to ask me to GIVE this? To my people? For my glory? (ASK is the second to last chapter of this book for a reason. More on that later too.)

During that trip, "The Father's going to GIVE it!" went to "The Father wants to GIVE it!" This dramatically changed how we prayed. It moved our prayers from uncertainty and doubt to confidence and thanksgiving. Now please understand that doesn't mean we began to control God with our prayers. No.

We began to trust God on higher levels. Jesus taught us to pray:

"Father, if you are willing, . . . I want your will to be done, not mine." –Luke 22:42 (NLT)

We prayed with bold faith, asking God to faithfully GIVE everything He brought before us. We did so with full surrender and submission to His will. As you will see in this book, sometimes the true GIFT lies in trusting God enough to ask, regardless of whether we receive. The GIFT is experiencing God. It's knowing His Word, heart, will, and way. It's having confident hope and trust to let Him decide when and how He GIVES His GIFTS to us. It is a GIFT to simply see: the Father's going to GIVE it!

"The Father's going to GIVE it" changes EVERYTHING! Let this sink in...

GIVE.

GIVE it.

The Father.

He.

He is going to GIVE it.

The Father's going to GIVE it!

As soon as I returned from my trip, God said: "Now, I want you to go write down everything in my Word that I promise to GIVE."

My team and I started making a list of every scripture in the Bible where God promises to GIVE something. It took us months! The more we wrote down, the more we found. I was truly blown away as we discovered more and more of what God has promised to GIVE us. I was also sad that I had never seen the extent of God's GIFTS like this before.

I suspect you have not either.

RIGHT NOW

Right now, there's a young mother or father working for money instead of staying home with their children because they're doubting that The Father's going to GIVE it.

Right now, a business owner has hit a ceiling in the growth of his company. He can't afford to finance the vision God has GIVEN him. Despite trying everything he knows to secure more capital for its expansion, he's stuck because he never realized he could depend on the GIFTS of God.

Right now, someone senses God's call to go on a mission trip. They diligently study it, discover the associated costs, and abruptly halt in their tracks, feeling overwhelmed by the financial burden. They believe in the saying "God's will, God's bill," but it never occurs to them to trust God for His GIFTS.

Right now, someone dreams of attending college but is discouraged by the daunting cost. Affording college tuition appears utterly impossible to them. Sadly, they've never been taught to rely on the GIFTS of God.

These real-life examples are sad, and what's even more disheartening is that they involve followers of Jesus. All of these individuals know Jesus, have received forGIVEness, and are covered by His blood. However, they have never been taught to recognize and rely on the GIFTS of God. (Notice GIVE is even in the middle of forGIVEness. Look for them and you will see God's GIFTS everywhere!)

Many believers have limited knowledge of God's GIFTS, and only a few live in total dependence on them. Unfortunately, this is not commonly taught as it should be. That is, until now!

This book publishes the list of everything God promises to GIVE us in the Bible. Here is your opportunity to see and hear for yourself the very Word of God. When Romans 8:32 (NLT) says: "Since he did not spare even his own Son but GAVE him up for us all, won't he also GIVE us everything else?" –He means EVERYTHING!

We have intentionally used   to highlight every scripture. Be purposeful about reading through each scripture. It is the scripture that God promises won't return void. Only the scripture bears fruit. Don't skip or rush through the scriptures. Allow God time to speak every GIFT He promises to GIVE.

Come, let's go on this discovery tour together. You will immediately begin to think differently, pray differently, live differently and GIVE differently.

The world is yet to see what will happen when the people of God, together, all live with confident expectancy that The Father's going to GIVE it!

Get ready for God to blow your mind. Welcome to GIFTS.

01 | GIFTS

Throughout this book, I've made a deliberate choice to capitalize certain words: **GIFT, GIVE, GIVES,** and **GIVEN.** I did this to highlight just how frequently these words appear in God's Word. I've experienced firsthand that it's possible to study the Word, yet miss the profound reality and revelation of God's GIFTS.

Soon, you too will see that the Bible is filled with GIFTS from God.

> "GIFT" translated into Hebrew is "matana," and in Greek, it is "dórea."

> "GIFTS" appears approximately 80 times in the NLT Bible.

> "GIVE" – in Hebrew is "natan," and in Greek, "didomi."

> "GIVE" appears approximately 1,073 times in the NLT Bible.

> "GIVES" – in Hebrew, it's "natan or notenn," in Greek, "dosis/dinei."

"GIVES" appears approximately 111 times in the NLT Bible.

"GIVEN"– in Hebrew is "natun/nathiyn" and in Greek, it's "dedoménos."

"GIVEN" appears approximately 754 times in the NLT Bible.

We organized all these scriptures into six categories:

1. Land

2. Life

3. Family

4. Increase

5. Empowerment

6. Everything

During my study, I noticed three things:

1. There are more verses about God GIVING us land than anything else.

2. The word YOU is included all throughout God's GIFTS.

3. The word ASK is also included in God's GIFTS.

You'll see this laid out in the chapters of this book:

Chapter 1: Gifts

Chapter 2: You

Chapter 3: Land

Chapter 4: Life

Chapter 5: Family

Chapter 6: Increase

Chapter 7: Empowerment

Chapter 8: Everything

Chapter 9: Ask

Chapter 10: Depend

In addition to these, *thousands* of verses declare God's GIFTS even without using the word GIVES.

For example:

> "And we have received God's Spirit (not the world's spirit), so we can know the wonderful things God has freely GIVEN us."
> –1 Corinthians 2:12 (NLT)

> "Thank God for this GIFT too wonderful for words!" –2 Corinthians 9:15 (NLT)

> "Whatever is good and perfect is a GIFT coming down to us from God our Father, who created all the lights in the heavens. He never changes or casts a shifting shadow." –James 1:17 (NLT)

These facts highlight the vital importance of life-changing discipleship. Can you see how every follower of Christ should understand and put them into practice in their lives?

This book doesn't revolve around the notions of entitlement or attempting to control God. It also doesn't solely emphasize materialistic GIFTS. A genuine GIFT is undeserved, without any strings attached, and without any manipulation of return. A true GIFT remains just that – a GIFT.

> James 1:17 (NLT) says, "Whatever is good and perfect is a GIFT coming down to us from God our Father."

God's GIFTS are good and perfect. They are freely GIVEN, devoid of any hidden agendas or attempts to secure something in return. These GIFTS from God are genuinely unconditional. It honors Him when we understand, expect, and receive His GIFTS. Our reliance on His GIFTS rather than our own abilities is a profound way to honor God. In the next chapter, you will see God's GIFTS are for YOU.

02 | YOU

One of the potential tragedies of this book would be to agree that God desires to GIVE to everyone else but YOU. It takes faith to believe God wants to GIVE to others. It takes greater faith to believe God wants to GIVE GIFTS to you.

Unfortunately, some believers even argue that God's promises to His people in the Bible are not for the church today. This is not biblical. If God had intended to draw the line all the verses about GIFTS would include, "GIFTS I gave them", but as you'll see He clearly says, "GIFTS I GIVE you." The word "you" is overwhelmingly prevalent.

As we truly study all the verses in the Bible where God promises to GIVE something, one of the words you'll commonly find is the word: YOU. This isn't an accident. God is intentional.

It is no coincidence that verses about GIFTS do not often use the word: them.

Here's the truth. All throughout the Bible, you will see God using the word YOU along with the word GIFTS. God says:

I will GIVE to YOU.

This land I GIVE YOU.

I will GIVE YOU everything.

YOU means you. Don't accept some words but reject others. God didn't make any mistake, nor is He a God of confusion. God doesn't say "you" but mean "them" or "others."

If you read this book seeing God's GIFTS but turn a blind eye to the word you, then you'll only be accepting half truth. The whole truth is God promises to GIVE to you.

It is my prayer that by the end of this book, you too will SEE all God promises to GIVE to you. I pray you will fall on your face and worship God as The GIVER He has always been. Unfortunately, the church has not always honored God as The GIVER, but YOU will after reading this book.

In my first book, *Audacious Generosity: How to Experience, Receive, and GIVE More Than You*

Ever Thought Possible, God had me establish that God's "more" is always more of Him and more for Him. Nothing has protected me from entitlement, corruption, and greed more than this. I encourage you to affirm the same. God's more is more of Himself and more for Himself. This frees you to receive the GIFTS of God.

If we add the number of times "YOU" is included, such as "into the land I will GIVE you"...

- **You** occurs **14,399** times in the English Standard Version.

- **You** occurs **14,480** times in the New King James Version.

- **You** occurs **2,616** times in the King James Version–**11,917** if you count you, thou, or thee

Rest assured, as the world's best Father, God sees *you* today. You are highly valuable to Him. One of my favorite verses is Matthew 7:11 (NLT):

> "So if you sinful people know how to GIVE good GIFTS to your children, how much more will your heavenly Father GIVE good GIFTS to those who ask him."

What kind of Father would God be if He talked all throughout the Bible about GIFTS but never attached the word YOU? One of the greatest ways you can honor God is by allowing Him to speak to YOU. His whole pursuit is an intimate love relationship with you. He commits to YOU . . .

> " . . . when you pray, I will listen." –Jeremiah 29:12 (NLT)

What an incredible GIFT! Likewise, God seeks your wholehearted affection as you prioritize your pursuit of His kingdom and righteousness. When you make seeking God your primary responsibility, incredible things unfold in your life.

> "If you look for me wholeheartedly, you will find me." –Jeremiah 29:13 (NLT)

> "Seek the Kingdom of God above all else, and live righteously, and he will GIVE you everything you need." –Matthew 6:33 (NLT)

> Jesus refers to God's GIFT, saying, "'If you only knew the GIFT God has for you and who you are speaking to, you would ask me, and I would GIVE you living water.'" –John 4:10 (NLT)

God's presence is His most valuable GIFT. Accepting this opens the door to incredible rewards!

> "And it is impossible to please God without faith. Anyone who wants to come to him must believe that God exists and that he rewards those who sincerely seek him." –Hebrews 11:6 (NLT)

While it's true God loves to GIVE us His GIFTS, it honors him for us to seek Him, not just His GIFTS. As we seek Him, He promises to GIVE us everything we need.

God's GIFTS to you are endless. He asks us:

> "What do you have that God hasn't GIVEN you? And if everything you have is from God, why boast as though it were not a GIFT?" –1 Corinthians 4:7 (NLT)

When it comes to GIFTS, God's Word is very direct:

> "No one can receive anything unless God GIVES it from heaven." –John 3:27 (NLT)

God asks us:

> "Since he did not spare even his own Son but GAVE him up for us all, won't he also GIVE us everything else?" –Romans 8:32 (NLT)

God *promises* GIFTS:

> "The Spirit of God, who raised Jesus from the dead, lives in you. And just as God raised Christ Jesus from the dead, he will GIVE life to your mortal bodies by this same Spirit living within you." –Romans 8:11 (NLT)

God wants you to read these verses for yourself, not only for others. God's GIFTS are for YOU.

Take courage! The enemy of God doesn't want you to see these scriptures of everything God promises to GIVE you. Satan knows that as long as you depend on yourself instead of the GIFTS of God, then you will live limited instead of limitless lives.

Nothing slows the fulfillment of God's redemptive mission on earth more than this! Perhaps you already fear, "Will this lead me to entitlement, corruption, or greed?" God has called us to be led by faith, not by fear. Trust God to protect you from entitlement, corruption, and greed. Don't avoid God's Word because of fear. Instead, receive God's Word with faith. Be a believer.

This includes allowing God to say the word "you."

Allow me to point out something. All throughout the Bible, God calls us to focus on others. God's Word is for all 195 nations! God's promises to GIVE extend to every nation, tribe, people, and language. This is good news for all people. God doesn't teach us to focus on me, me, me, but them, them, them. The enemy will use this to trick us into believing God's GIFTS are for others and not for us. Here's the test of our faith: You focus on the nations, others, all people, and trust God to focus on you.

Just because God trains us to focus on Him and others doesn't mean He doesn't promise to GIVE to you. He does! Allowing him to say "you" will increase your faith in God giving to others through you.

Try this:

Does God want you to GIVE? Yes or no?

Does God want to GIVE to you? Yes or no?

All believers expect God wants them to GIVE. Few believers expect God to GIVE to them. What kind of

Father expects his children to GIVE without giving to them? In my book, Audacious Generosity, God had me declare: God is the GIVER and giving depends on what God puts into your hands. This order is very important! First, God GIVES to YOU. Because of that he calls you to GIVE to others. If you refuse to accept that God desires to GIVE to YOU it will limit you allowing Him to GIVE to others through YOU.

Jesus says, "It is more blessed to GIVE than to receive" (Acts 20:35 NLT). As we focus on GIVING to others, God GIVES to us. His GIFTS are for YOU too.

Let God say "you." "You" means YOU. Receive it and worship in humble thanksGIVing.

Told you! Once you accept God as The GIVER, you start seeing His GIFTS everywhere! Even thanksGIVing results from God's GIFTS!

As we're about to see, God has a lot to say about GIVING you land.

03 | LAND

Did you know that God talks more about giving us land than even forGIVEness of sin? What is He doing? Now, I'm not talking about a literal plot of dirt. Most Christians today don't even own land. So, what is He saying?

Land is like an endless treasure trove of GIFTS from God. Think about it: every meal we enjoy comes from the land. And it's not just about food. The land GIVES us plants, and those plants GIVE us oxygen. Our next breath, that deep inhale and exhale we don't even think about, it's all because of the land.

> "He will GIVE you lush pasture land for your livestock, and you yourselves will have all you want to eat." –Deuteronomy 11:15 (NLT)

Now, here's something to ponder: at any GIVEN moment, somewhere across the globe, people are actually fighting over land. It's that valuable and essential. And you know what the Bible says about this? It tells us that the earth – which is the land, and everything on it, were all GIVEN by Jesus and for Jesus.

> "God created everything through him [Jesus], and nothing was created except through him."
> –John 1:3 (NLT)

The land we walk on, the food we eat, the air we breathe – it's all connected back to this bigger plan and purpose. So let's start at the beginning of the Bible in Genesis 1.

God created land before humans. Picture this: On the third day of creation, God formed the land, and brought life to what was empty. Just as that life sprang from the barren earth, centuries later, Jesus rose from the grave. His resurrection breathed life into what was dead.

Allow me to point out seven reasons land is an incredible GIFT from God for you:

1. It Represents Your Life!

We are made from the land. God created man from clay. We come from and return to the land.

> "Then God said, 'Let the waters beneath the sky flow together into one place, so dry ground may appear.' And that is what happened." –Genesis 1:9 (NLT)

"Then the Lord God formed the man from the dust of the ground. He breathed the breath of life into the man's nostrils, and the man became a living person." –Genesis 2:7 (NLT)

2. It GIVES You a Future.

Creating land wasn't just shaping the world; it set the stage for life's future. On days five and six, God's divine power brought countless creatures into being, both humans and animals. The abundant life on land displays God's beauty, creativity, strength, and power—a clear sign of His existence.

"For ever since the world was created, people have seen the earth and sky. Through everything God made, they can clearly see his invisible qualities—his eternal power and divine nature. So they have no excuse for not knowing God." –Romans 1:20 (NLT)

3. He Desires to be with You Now and Forever.

Initially, God dwelled with Adam and Eve on the land, but their disobedience led to their departure from the garden, where the Tree of Life once provided shade. It's comforting to know that God has a plan for us to one day live with Him again by the Tree of Life in the New Heaven and Earth! When sin is gone, we can be with God no matter where we are on this land.

Jesus came to be with us in the land of Israel, and now His Holy Spirit lives in us.

He compared our hearts to the soil, where He and His Word can grow and flourish.

The Parable of the Sower in the Bible, found in Matthew 13, Mark 4, and Luke 8, pictures our hearts as different types of soil. Seeds (which represent God's Word) fall on various kinds of ground (land). Just like seeds grow well in good soil, the message of God grows in people who are open and ready to understand it. The story shows that when our hearts are like good soil, open and receptive, God's teachings can grow and flourish in us.

4. He GIVES You a Place to Live.

The Lord owns the heavens, but He has GIVEN the earth to everyone.

> "The heavens belong to the Lord, but he has GIVEN the earth to all humanity." –Psalm 115:16 (NLT)

God's promise to keep His people safe in their land, ensuring they won't be displaced again, shows His protective and lasting love for His chosen ones.

> "'I will firmly plant them there in their own land. They will never again be uprooted from the land I have GIVEN them,' says the Lord your God." –Amos 9:15 (NLT)

> "I, the Sovereign Lord, will gather you back from the nations where you have been scattered, and I will GIVE you the land of Israel once again." –Ezekiel 11:17 (NLT)

He gave towns for the Israelites' families and their livestock. It's as if God was saying, "Here's a safe place for your loved ones and all that you own." This wasn't just about land; it was about a home, a community, a place where life could flourish and grow.

"Your wives, children, and numerous livestock, however, may stay behind in the towns I have GIVEN you." –Deuteronomy 3:19 (NLT)

When the walls of Jericho fell, it was more than just a military victory. Joshua told the people to shout because the Lord had GIVEN them the town. It's a powerful reminder that the places we live in are GIFTS from God, places where He wants us to thrive and make a life.

"The seventh time around, as the priests sounded the long blast on their horns, Joshua commanded the people, 'Shout! For the Lord has GIVEN you the town!'" –Joshua 6:16 (NLT)

Joshua 8:7 adds another layer to this. Here, the Israelites were about to take over a town, and it was clear that their success was because the Lord was giving it to them. Every place we settle down, every community we build, is not just our doing; it's a blessing, a GIFT from God.

" . . . you will jump up from your ambush and take possession of the town, for the Lord your God will GIVE it to you." –Joshua 8:7 (NLT)

So, when we think about where we live, whether it's a bustling city or a quiet countryside, it's amazing to realize that God has GIVEN us these places. They're not just spaces on a map; they're homes, communities, and opportunities that God has provided for us to live, grow, and be part of something bigger.

5. He Keeps His Promises.

God is committed to giving a specific and meaningful inheritance to His people.

> "I will GIVE you the land of Canaan as your special possession." –Psalm 105:11 (NLT) and 1 Chronicles 16:18 (NLT)

God's promise to Abraham and his descendants wasn't about following a set of rules. It was all about having a deep, trusting relationship with God through faith. This verse really drives home the point that faith is at the core of God's promises and blessings.

> "Clearly, God's promise to GIVE the whole earth to Abraham and his descendants was based not on his obedience to God's law, but on a right relationship with God that comes by faith." –Romans 4:13 (NLT)

41

We can celebrate God's unwavering commitment to His promises!

> "When he had proved himself faithful, you made a covenant with him to GIVE him and his descendants the land of the Canaanites, Hittites, Amorites, Perizzites, Jebusites, and Girgashites. And you have done what you promised, for you are always true to your word." –Nehemiah 9:8 (NLT)

God's promise to Abraham and his descendants is like a journey that hasn't reached its final destination yet. You see, the complete possession of the land, as God pledged to Abraham, Isaac, and Jacob, hasn't happened entirely. If we take a closer look at the borders outlined in Genesis 12:15 and Exodus 23, we'll realize that the Promised Land extends even beyond what we often think. It includes regions like the West Bank, Gaza Strip, parts of Lebanon, Syria, and Jordan.

Now, the grand finale of this promise is expected during the Millennial Kingdom and Messianic Age. This incredible moment will mark the regathering, rejuvenation, reign, and the ultimate restoration of Israel. And it's not just for Israel; it's a blessing for all believers because blessing Abraham's descendants leads to blessings for everyone else. The Promised Land isn't just a symbolic concept; it's a tangible reminder of our trust in God's Word.

And here's the wonderful thing: God keeps His promises. Sometimes they come to pass quickly, and other times they unfold over time, but they always happen perfectly according to His divine plan. So, let's trust, and look forward to the amazing fulfillment of God's promises!

6. You Can Find Rest.

In Israel, even the land gets a breather during the Shemitah – that's a seven-year "rest" period when no crops are grown. Just like that, God promises to GIVE rest to the people He loves. It's a beautiful reminder that rest is part of God's plan for us too, not just for the land. So, when life gets a bit overwhelming, remember, God's got your back, and He's all about giving you that much-needed rest.

> "Remember what Moses, the servant of the Lord commanded you: 'The Lord your God is GIVING you a place of rest. He has GIVEN you this LAND.'" –Joshua 1:13 (NLT)

"Praise the Lord who has GIVEN rest to his people, Israel, just as he promised. Not one word has failed of all the wonderful promises he GAVE through his servant Moses." –1 Kings 8:56 (NLT)

" . . . until the Lord GIVES them rest, and until they, too, possess the land the Lord your God is GIVING them. Only then may you return and settle here on the east side of the Jordan River in the land that Moses, the servant of the Lord, assigned to you." –Joshua 1:15 (NLT)

"And now the Lord your God has GIVEN the other tribes rest, as he promised them. So go back home to the land that Moses, the servant of the Lord, GAVE you as your possession on the east side of the Jordan River." –Joshua 22:4 (NLT)

7. It Teaches the Importance of Faithfulness.

In the "Land Covenant" conversation in Deuteronomy 29 and 30, God basically laid it out for Israel. We can think of His message as, "I'm giving you this awesome land, but here's the catch: you've got to obey Me and do what I say if you want to thrive in it."

Moses warned them that if they played by the rules and obeyed God, they'd continue to enjoy blessings. But if they didn't, they'd lose the land and all the benefits.

Unfortunately, the Israelites didn't hold up their end of the bargain, which led to them getting them kicked out of the land. Tough lessons from history, right?

> "But as surely as the Lord your God has GIVEN you the good things he promised, he will also bring disaster on you if you disobey him. He will completely destroy you from the good land he has GIVEN you." –Joshua 23:15 (NLT)

God never breaks His promises. The Land Covenant, for example, is all about the eternal promise He made. He plans to save His people, and it involves giving them brand-new hearts and spirits. Plus, He's going to bring them all back to the land, and they'll be there forever.

> "Then the surrounding nations that survive will know that I, the Lord, have rebuilt the ruins and replanted the wasteland. For I, the Lord, have spoken, and I will do what I say." –Ezekiel 36:36 (NLT)

> "'I will firmly plant them there in their own land. They will never again be uprooted from the land I have GIVEN them,' says the Lord your God." –Amos 9:15 (NLT)

LAND is an invaluable GIFT from God. Actually, it doesn't matter whose name is on the deed. All LAND belongs to God. He's GIVEN it to us. It sustains our LIFE. In the next chapter, we will see how God specifically promises to GIVE us the GIFT of LIFE.

04 | LIFE

God is incredibly generous, showering us with many GIFTS. He doesn't just create life; He renews it every day. His GIFTS include authority, forGIVEness, grace, and provision for our needs. Through Jesus, we receive forGIVEness and the promise of eternal life. God's generosity covers all aspects of our lives, from hope to salvation and security. His generosity knows no bounds!

God isn't a distant creator; He's actively breathing life into every creature. It's not just about creating life; it's about continuously fueling it. Isn't that amazing? That every living thing gets its breath from God!

> "O Lord, you are the God who GIVES breath to all creatures." –Numbers 27:16 (NLT)

The scriptures paint a vivid picture of God, not only giving life, but renewing it. It's like each day, with every sunrise, God is refreshing the world, giving us new life and new opportunities. It's not just a one-off act; it's an ongoing, daily renewal. Every little thing that grows, every creature that's born, these are all part of God's constant act of renewal.

"When you GIVE them your breath, life is created, and you renew the face of the earth."
–Psalm 104:30 (NLT)

Consider the words of Isaiah. This verse is mind-blowing! It says God created everything – the heavens, the earth, and all of us walking around on it. The same breath that stretches out the heavens is the one that GIVES life to every person on earth. What a beautiful idea! God's GIFT of life is for everyone, everywhere. It's a universal, unending GIFT.

"God, the Lord, created the heavens and stretched them out.
He created the earth and everything in it.
He GIVES breath to everyone,
life to everyone who walks the earth" –Isaiah 42:5 (NLT)

Every breath is a GIFT, and every day is a chance to appreciate the One who gave us this life.

Look at other GIFTS that He has waiting for you:

Authority

1. God GIVES authority to Jesus.

   "For you have GIVEN him authority over everyone. He GIVES eternal life to each one you have GIVEN him." –John 17:2 (NLT)

2. God GIVES authority to those who follow Jesus.

   "Look, I have GIVEN you authority over all the power of the enemy, and you can walk among snakes and scorpions and crush them. Nothing will injure you." –Luke 10:19, (NLT)

   "Through Christ, God has GIVEN us the privilege and authority as apostles to tell Gentiles everywhere what God has done for them, so that they will believe and obey him, bringing glory to his name." –Romans 1:5 (NLT)

   "I may seem to be boasting too much about the authority GIVEN to us by the Lord." –2 Corinthians 10:8 (NLT)

"To all who are victorious, who obey me to the very end, To them I will GIVE authority over all the nations." –Revelation 2:26 (NLT)

3. Authority is GIVEN to specific individuals in the context of leadership and faithful service to God.

"I will dress him in your royal robes and will GIVE him your title and your authority. And he will be a father to the people of Jerusalem and Judah. I will GIVE him the key to the house of David—the highest position in the royal court. When he opens doors, no one will be able to close them; when he closes doors, no one will be able to open them." –Isaiah 22:21-22 (NLT)

"This is what the Lord of Heaven's Armies says: If you follow my ways and carefully serve me, then you will be GIVEN authority over my Temple and its courtyards. I will let you walk among these others standing here." –Zechariah 3:7 (NLT)

Blood

The life of a body is in its blood. God instructed Old Testament worshipers about the use of blood on the altar for purification, making people right with Him. When Jesus sacrificed Himself on the cross, His perfect blood was made available to us.

> "For the life of the body is in its blood. I have GIVEN you the blood on the altar to purify you, making you right with the Lord. It is the blood, GIVEN in exchange for a life, that makes purification possible." –Leviticus 17:11 (NLT)

Body

At the Last Supper, Jesus took some bread, expressed gratitude to God, broke it, and gave it to His disciples, saying,

> "This is my body, which is GIVEN for you. Do this in remembrance of me." –Luke 22:19 (NLT)

He started the practice of communion to represent His sacrifice for believers' salvation. The breaking of bread symbolizes Jesus' body GIVEN for humanity's redemption, and believers are told to remember this whenever they have communion.

Imagine various plants growing from different seeds. It's like God's power transforming each seed into a new body. Look at how diverse God's creation is! He GIVES each seed a special body, revealing His intentional and creative design for all living things.

> "Then God GIVES it the new body he wants it to have. A different plant grows from each kind of seed." –1 Corinthians 15:38 (NLT)

Fame

When Solomon asked for wisdom, God gave him that and more. He also promised extraordinary favor and blessings!

> "And I will also GIVE you what you did not ask for—riches and fame! No other king in all the world will be compared to you for the rest of your life!" –1 Kings 3:13 (NLT)

God spoke to the people of Jerusalem, assuring them of comfort, restoration, and vindication after they went through tough times and persecution.

"And I will deal severely with all who have oppressed you. I will save the weak and helpless ones; I will bring together those who were chased away. I will GIVE glory and fame to my former exiles, wherever they have been mocked and shamed." –Zephaniah 3:19 (NLT)

Food

God generously provides for His people. Whether it's from the time of the Israelites in Exodus or taking care of orphans, widows, and foreigners with food and clothing, God ensures everyone has what they need. He remembers His promises and takes care of those who respect Him.

"Then Moses added, 'The Lord will GIVE you meat to eat in the evening and bread to satisfy you in the morning, for he has heard all your complaints against him. What have we done? Yes, your complaints are against the Lord, not against us.'" –Exodus 16:8 (NLT)

"Then God said, 'Look! I have GIVEN you every seed-bearing plant throughout the earth and all the fruit trees for your food.'" –Genesis 1:29 (NLT)

"The Israelites were puzzled when they saw it. 'What is it?' they asked each other. They had no idea what it was. And Moses told them, 'It is the food the Lord has GIVEN you to eat.'" –Exodus 16:15 (NLT)

"He ensures that orphans and widows receive justice. He shows love to the foreigners living among you and GIVES them food and clothing." –Deuteronomy 10:18 (NLT)

"They all depend on you to GIVE them food as they need it." –Psalm 104:27 (NLT)

"He GIVES food to those who fear him; he always remembers his covenant." –Psalm 111:5 (NLT)

"He GIVES food to every living thing. His faithful love endures forever." –Psalm 136:25 (NLT)

"The eyes of all look to you in hope; you GIVE them their food as they need it." –Psalm 145:15 (NLT)

"He GIVES food to the wild animals and feeds the young ravens when they cry." –Psalm 147:9 (NLT)

"He is a merciful creditor, not keeping the items GIVEN as security by poor debtors. He does not rob the poor but instead GIVES food to the hungry and provides clothes for the needy." –Ezekiel 18:7 (NLT)

"He does not exploit the poor, but instead is fair to debtors and does not rob them. He GIVES food to the hungry and provides clothes for the needy." –Ezekiel 18:16 (NLT)

" . . . To everyone who is victorious I will GIVE fruit from the tree of life in the paradise of God." –Revelation 2:7 (NLT)

ForGIVEness of Sin

Through Jesus Christ, God generously forGIVES, a stark contrast to the impact of Adam's sin that caused death.

"But there is a great difference between Adam's sin and God's gracious GIFT. For the sin of this one man, Adam, brought death to many. But even greater is God's wonderful grace and his GIFT of forGIVEness to many through this other man, Jesus Christ." –Romans 5:15 (NLT)

Garments

God gave instructions to Moses on how to make special clothing for the priests who served in the Tabernacle. The materials and colors used for these garments highlighted their importance and significance.

> "So GIVE them fine linen cloth, gold thread, and blue, purple, and scarlet thread." –Exodus 28:5 (NLT)

Grace

Grace is a GIFT we receive. We don't earn it or deserve it. It's a way of showing kindness and love without expecting anything in return. And God does that for us, giving us good things and forGIVEness, even when we mess up.

> "For the LORD God is our sun and our shield. He GIVES us grace and glory. The LORD will withhold no good thing from those who do what is right." –Psalm 84:11 (NLT)

> "May God our Father and the Lord Jesus Christ GIVE you grace and peace." –2 Corinthians 1:2 (NLT)

"And they will pray for you with deep affection because of the overflowing grace God has GIVEN to you." –2 Corinthians 9:14 (NLT)

"May God the Father and our Lord Jesus Christ GIVE you grace and peace." –Galatians 1:3 (NLT)

"And he GIVES grace generously. As the Scriptures say, 'God opposes the proud but GIVES grace to the humble.'" –James 4:6 (NLT)

"In the same way, you who are younger must accept the authority of the elders. And all of you, dress yourselves in humility as you relate to one another, for 'God opposes the proud but GIVES grace to the humble.'" –1 Peter 5:5 (NLT)

Health

God's love for us is so deep that He not only cares for our spiritual well-being but also our physical health. Even when we feel like outcasts, when no one else seems to care, God is there, ready to restore our health and mend our wounds. His healing touch is evidence of His compassion and care for us in every part of our lives.

> "'I will GIVE you back your health and heal your wounds,' says the Lord. 'For you are called an outcast—'Jerusalem for whom no one cares.'" –Jeremiah 30:17 (NLT)

Heart

God's love and grace reach deep into our souls, giving us new hearts that recognize Him as Lord. This leads us to wholeheartedly devote ourselves to Him. We become His people, and He becomes our God. His intention is for us to worship Him with unity and purpose, benefiting both us and future generations. God promises to replace our hardened hearts with soft, responsive ones, giving us a fresh start and renewing our relationship with Him.

> "I will GIVE them hearts that recognize me as the Lord. They will be my people, and I will be their God, for they will return to me wholeheartedly." –Jeremiah 24:7 (NLT)

> "And I will GIVE them one heart and one purpose: to worship me forever, for their own

good and for the good of all their descendants."
–Jeremiah 32:39 (NLT)

"And I will GIVE them singleness of heart and put a new spirit within them. I will take away their stony, stubborn heart and GIVE them a tender, responsive heart." –Ezekiel 11:19 (NLT)

"I will GIVE you a new heart." –Ezekiel 36:26 (NLT)

Hope

The scriptures GIVE us hope and encouragement, teaching us valuable lessons. They help us patiently wait for God's promises to come true. God has GIVEN His chosen ones a confident hope that lights up our hearts and helps us understand our glorious inheritance. God's promises continue to GIVE us the hope we need in life.

"Such things were written in the Scriptures long ago to teach us. And the Scriptures GIVE us hope and encouragement as we wait patiently for God's promises to be fulfilled." –Romans 15:4 (NLT)

"I pray that your hearts will be flooded with light so that you can understand the confident hope he has GIVEN to those he called—his holy people who are his rich and glorious inheritance." –Ephesians 1:18 (NLT)

Life

God *is* life; He GIVES and sustains it. Obeying His instructions can lead to a long life. The Spirit of God provides our daily breath. Trusting in Him brings rewards and rescue. God fulfills our needs, and through Christ, we find new life. God is the GIVER of life in every way.

"There will be no miscarriages or infertility in your land, and I will GIVE you long, full lives." –Exodus 23:26 (NLT)

"Look now; I myself am he! There is no other god but me! I am the one who kills and GIVES life; I am the one who wounds and heals; no one can be rescued from my powerful hand!" –Deuteronomy 32:39 (NLT)

"The Lord GIVES both death and life; he brings some down to the grave but raises others up."
–1 Samuel 2:6 (NLT)

"And if you follow me and obey my decrees and my commands as your father, David, did, I will GIVE you a long life." –1 Kings 3:14 (NLT)

"For the Spirit of God has made me, and the breath of the Almighty GIVES me life." –Job 33:4 (NLT)

"But each day the Lord pours his unfailing love upon me, and through each night I sing his songs, praying to God who GIVES me life."
–Psalm 42:8 (NLT)

"Seventy years are GIVEN to us! Some even live to eighty. But even the best years are filled with pain and trouble; soon they disappear, and we fly away." –Psalm 90:10 (NLT)

"Because you trusted me, I will GIVE you your life as a reward. I will rescue you and keep you safe. I, the Lord, have spoken!" –Jeremiah 39:18 (NLT)

"Are you seeking great things for yourself? Don't do it! I will bring great disaster upon all these people; but I will GIVE you your life as a reward wherever you go. I, the Lord, have spoken!" –Jeremiah 45:5 (NLT)

"Humans can reproduce only human life, but the Holy Spirit GIVES birth to spiritual life." –John 3:6 (NLT)

"For just as the Father GIVES life to those he raises from the dead, so the Son GIVES life to anyone he wants."–John 5:21 (NLT)

"The thief's purpose is to steal and kill and destroy. My purpose is to GIVE them a rich and satisfying life." –John 10:10 (NLT)

" . . . He himself GIVES life and breath to everything, and he satisfies every need." –Acts 17:25 (NLT)

"And Christ lives within you, so even though your body will die because of sin, the Spirit GIVES you life because you have been made right with God." –Romans 8:10 (NLT)

"The Spirit of God, who raised Jesus from the dead, lives in you. And just as God raised Christ Jesus from the dead, he will GIVE life to your mortal bodies by this same Spirit living within you." –Romans 8:11 (NLT)

"Just as everyone dies because we all belong to Adam, everyone who belongs to Christ will be GIVEN new life." –1 Corinthians 15:22 (NLT)

"He has enabled us to be ministers of his new covenant. This is a covenant not of written laws, but of the Spirit. The old written covenant ends in death; but under the new covenant, the Spirit GIVES life." –2 Corinthians 3:6 (NLT)

Morning Star

The "morning star" represents a special blessing or a share in the authority and glory of Jesus Christ. It points to a unique GIFT or reward that will be GIVEN to those who overcome and remain faithful to Him.

"They will have the same authority I received from my Father, and I will also GIVE them the morning star!" –Revelation 2:28 (NLT)

New Song

God GIVES us a new song, a joyful hymn of praise. It's a song that celebrates His goodness and the amazing things He does. When we sing this song, others will see God's works and put their trust in Him.

> "He has GIVEN me a new song to sing, a hymn of praise to our God. Many will see what he has done and be amazed. They will put their trust in the Lord." –Psalm 40:3 (NLT)

New Way

God has graciously provided us with a new way, and it fills us with confidence and boldness. This new path, GIVEN to us by God's mercy, empowers us to never GIVE up.

> "Since this new way GIVES us such confidence, we can be very bold." –2 Corinthians 3:12 (NLT)

> "Therefore, since God in his mercy has GIVEN us this new way, we never GIVE up." –2 Corinthians 4:1 (NLT)

Rest

1. Rest from work

Sometimes we work so hard, from early morning till late at night, and we worry so much about making ends meet. But here's the beautiful thing: God GIVES us rest. And when we're feeling tired and down, God promises to refresh us and fill us with joy. Imagine a day when God will GIVE us rest from all our troubles, sorrow, and fear. That's something to look forward to!

> "It is useless for you to work so hard from early morning until late at night, anxiously working for food to eat; for God GIVES rest to his loved ones." –Psalm 127:2 (NLT)

> "Then Jesus said, 'Come to me, all of you who are weary and carry heavy burdens, and I will GIVE you rest.'" –Matthew 11:28 (NLT)

> "It is useless for you to work so hard from early morning until late at night, anxiously working for food to eat; for God GIVES rest to his loved ones." –Psalm 127:2 (NLT)

"In that wonderful day when the Lord GIVES his people rest from sorrow and fear, from slavery and chains, . . . " –Isaiah 14:3 (NLT)

"For I have GIVEN rest to the weary and joy to the sorrowing." –Jeremiah 31:25 (NLT)

2. Rest from enemies

God GIVES us rest from our enemies when we enter new "lands" or opportunities, which He also GIVES us. He personally goes with us, assuring us that everything will be fine. He's got our back! This promise has been kept throughout history, just as God assured Moses and King David. Even in difficult times, God offers rest and protection, leading us to peaceful places.

"But you will soon cross the Jordan River and live in the land the Lord your God is GIVING you. When he GIVES you rest from all your enemies and you're living safely in the land, . . . " –Deuteronomy 12:10 (NLT)

"Therefore, when the Lord your God has GIVEN you rest from all your enemies in the land he is GIVING you as a special possession, you must destroy the Amalekites and erase their

memory from under heaven. Never forget this!"
–Deuteronomy 25:19 (NLT)

"Remember what Moses, the servant of the Lord, commanded you: 'The Lord your God is GIVING you a place of rest. He has GIVEN you this land.'" –Joshua 1:13 (NLT)

" . . . until the Lord GIVES them rest, as he has GIVEN you rest, and until they, too, possess the land the Lord your God is GIVING them. Only then may you return and settle here on the east side of the Jordan River in the land that Moses, the servant of the Lord, assigned to you." –Joshua 1:15 (NLT)

"The Lord replied, 'I will personally go with you, Moses, and I will GIVE you rest—everything will be fine for you.'" –Exodus 33:14 (NLT)

"And now the Lord your God has GIVEN the other tribes rest, as he promised them. So go back home to the land that Moses, the servant of the Lord, GAVE you as your possession on the east side of the Jordan River." –Joshua 22:4 (NLT)

"The years passed, and the Lord had GIVEN the people of Israel rest from all their enemies." –Joshua 23:1 (NLT)

"When King David was settled in his palace and the Lord had GIVEN him rest from all the surrounding enemies . . . " –2 Samuel 7:1 (NLT)

" . . . starting from the time I appointed judges to rule my people Israel. And I will GIVE you rest from all your enemies. "'Furthermore, the Lord declares that he will make a house for you—a dynasty of kings!" –2 Samuel 7:11 (NLT)

"Praise the Lord who has GIVEN rest to his people Israel, just as he promised. Not one word has failed of all the wonderful promises he gave through his servant Moses." –1 Kings 8:56 (NLT)

"So Jehoshaphat's kingdom was at peace, for his God had GIVEN him rest on every side." –2 Chronicles 20:30 (NLT)

"This is what the Lord says: 'Those who survive the coming destruction will find blessings even in the barren land, for I will GIVE rest to the people of Israel.'" –Jeremiah 31:2 (NLT)

"But the one who redeems them is strong. His name is the Lord of Heaven's Armies. He will defend them and GIVE them rest again in Israel. But for the people of Babylon there will be no rest!" –Jeremiah 50:34 (NLT)

"Yes, I will GIVE them good pastureland on the high hills of Israel. There they will lie down in pleasant places and feed in the lush pastures of the hills." –Ezekiel 34:14 (NLT)

3. Rest as worship

God gave us a day of rest, showing His covenant and His role in making us holy. When we pause to rest and focus our thoughts upon God, we worship and honor Him. It's a way of demonstrating how important He is in our lives.

"Tell the people of Israel: 'Be careful to keep my Sabbath day, for the Sabbath is a sign of the covenant between me and you from generation to generation. It is GIVEN so you may know that I am the Lord, who makes you holy." –Exodus 31:13 (NLT)

Prophesy

God has an incredible way of giving us glimpses of the future through prophecy. You see, there was a moment when King Cyrus of Persia made a proclamation that had been foretold by the prophet Jeremiah. God whispered to Jeremiah, telling him what would happen, and then, in the first year of King Cyrus's reign, it all came true. It's amazing how God can stir the hearts of leaders to fulfill His prophecies, and it shows us that God's plans always come to pass, just as He said they would.

> "In the first year of King Cyrus of Persia, the Lord fulfilled the prophecy he had GIVEN through Jeremiah. He stirred the heart of Cyrus to put this proclamation in writing and to send it throughout his kingdom . . . " –Ezra 1:1 (NLT)

Protection

God shows His love and care by giving protection. He revived ancient Israel, giving them strength to rebuild His Temple, and restore the ruins. But He didn't stop there; He also provided them with a protective wall. It's a powerful reminder that God not only helps us rebuild what's broken, but also shields us from harm, ensuring our safety and well-being. His protection is a tangible expression of His love and grace.

> "He revived us so we could rebuild the Temple of our God and repair its ruins. He has GIVEN us a protective wall in Judah and Jerusalem."
> –Ezra 9:9b (NLT)

Salvation

God's GIFT of salvation is wonderful. When we believe, it's His grace that saves us, and we can't take credit or brag about it. It's not about our good deeds. He even promises a long life and His salvation. Remember the amazing sign He gave us when a virgin gave birth to Immanuel, which means "God is with us." There's simply no other way to be saved.

> "God saved you by his grace when you believed. And you can't take credit for this; it is a GIFT from God. Salvation is not a reward for the good things we have done, so none of us can boast about it." –Ephesians 2:8-9 (NLT)

> "I will reward them with a long life and GIVE them my salvation." –Psalm 91:16 (NLT)

"All right then, the Lord himself will GIVE you the sign. Look! The virgin will conceive a child! She will GIVE birth to a son and will call him Immanuel (which means 'God is with us')."
–Isaiah 7:14 (NLT)

"There is salvation in no one else! God has GIVEN no other name under heaven by which we must be saved." –Acts 4:12 (NLT)

Security

God GIVES us a sense of safety and protection, and offers us relief from the burdens of our struggles and hardships.

"He has GIVEN us security in this holy place. Our God has brightened our eyes and granted us some relief from our slavery." –Ezra 9:8b (NLT)

Supply

God's way of providing for us is like having a never-ending source of what we need. When He supplies, we gather and feel truly satisfied. He opens His hand to GIVE us what we require, and we find ourselves richly blessed and content. God generously takes care of His children!

> "When you supply it, they gather it. You open your hand to feed them, and they are richly satisfied." –Psalm 104:28 (NLT)

Water

God's way of giving water is miraculous. In the wilderness, when the Israelites were thirsty, God told Moses to gather the people, and He provided water from a well. He even made water flow from rocks like a gushing spring. God promises to GIVE rivers, fountains, and pools of water in various places, showing His limitless abundance. In the bigger picture, He's the Beginning and the End, offering the water of life to anyone who's thirsty, both physically and spiritually. It's amazing how God provides for our needs.

> "From there the Israelites traveled to Beer, which is the well where the Lord said to Moses, 'Assemble the people, and I will GIVE them water.'" –Numbers 21:16 (NLT)

"He split open the rocks in the wilderness to GIVE them water, as from a gushing spring." –Psalm 78:15 (NLT)

"I will open up rivers for them on the high plateaus. I will GIVE them fountains of water in the valleys. I will fill the desert with pools of water. Rivers fed by springs will flow across the parched ground." –Isaiah 41:18 (NLT)

"And he also said, 'It is finished! I am the Alpha and the Omega—the Beginning and the End. To all who are thirsty I will GIVE freely from the springs of the water of life." –Revelation 21:6 (NLT)

Just think. God has a solution for every need we encounter in life, and He's more than willing to share those resources with us. Whatever it is you're facing or seeking, don't hesitate to bring it to Him because He's got you covered. So, what's on your heart? What do you need today? It's a comforting thought to know that God is there, ready to provide for you in your times of need.

God desires to GIVE you LIFE. In the next chapter, we'll explore how God desires to GIVE you FAMILY.

05 | FAMILY

Biological Family

Families are close to God's heart. In fact, they were His idea in the first place. God is the GIVER of children and descendants. They are blessings from God, emphasizing His provision and grace in providing families. Family is where invisible love becomes visible.

> "He GIVES the childless woman a family, making her a happy mother. Praise the Lord!"
> –Psalm 113:9 (NLT)

You are part of something greater than just yourself. While your individual existence matters, your family shapes and defines you, giving you an identity beyond your name. Your position in the world is interconnected with various relationships, especially those within your family, which not only define you but also offer opportunities for personal growth.

Promised Family

God called Abraham and promised him countless descendants. He asked Abraham to leave his home and go to a land God would show him. God pledged to make him a great nation, and bless all nations through him.

> "And I will GIVE you so many descendants that, like the dust of the earth, they cannot be counted!" –Genesis 13:16 (NLT)

> "Then he added, 'I will GIVE you more descendants than you can count.'" –Genesis 16:10 (NLT)

> "I will make a covenant with you, by which I will guarantee to GIVE you countless descendants." –Genesis 17:2 (NLT)

> "I will cause your descendants to become as numerous as the stars of the sky, and I will GIVE them all these lands. And through your descendants all the nations of the earth will be blessed." –Genesis 26:4 (NLT)

God is faithful to His promises. Sarah experienced a miraculous conception at age ninety and gave birth to Isaac, fulfilling God's commitment to provide a son to Abraham and Sarah in their old age. In their case, God's promise did not rely on human ability, just as His promised miracles in our lives do not depend on our own capabilities.

> "And I will bless her and GIVE you a son from her! Yes, I will bless her richly, and she will become the mother of many nations. Kings of nations will be among her descendants." –Genesis 17:16 (NLT)

> "Who would have said to Abraham that Sarah would nurse a baby? Yet I have GIVEN Abraham a son in his old age!" –Genesis 21:7 (NLT)

Isaac was born. Then Isaac had a son named Jacob, who was sent by his parents to find a wife in their home country. Before he left, Isaac blessed Jacob, asking God to GIVE him many descendents. On his journey, he had a dream, and God reaffirmed the promise made to his grandfather.

> "May God Almighty bless you and GIVE you many children. And may your descendants multiply and become many nations!" –Genesis 28:3 (NLT)

Years later, we read this conversation between Jacob and his brother, Esau.

> "Then Esau looked at the women and children and asked, 'Who are these people with you?' 'These are the children God has graciously GIVEN to me, your servant,' Jacob replied."
> –Genesis 33:5 (NLT)

Even more years passed, and during those years, Jacob had twelve sons and one daughter. Although the family struggled, made poor choices, and endured broken lives, God's promise remained.

> "'Yes,' Joseph told him, 'these are the sons God has GIVEN me here in Egypt.' And Jacob said, 'Bring them closer to me, so I can bless them.'"
> –Genesis 48:9 (NLT)

Hundreds of years later, we still see the promise that's alive. God loves families! He GIVES children. God's blessings extend through generations.

> "He will love you and bless you, and he will GIVE you many children. He will GIVE fertility to your land and your animals." –Deuteronomy 7:13a (NLT)

The idea of God giving descendants is often linked to His promised covenant with individuals and nations, emphasizing the significance of God's relationship with His people.

> "And may the Lord GIVE you descendants by this young woman who will be like those of our ancestor Perez, the son of Tamar and Judah."
> –Ruth 4:12 (NLT)

God's Family

God didn't intend for you to journey through life in isolation. In fact, God dislikes loneliness. When He created humanity, He placed them in the perfect Garden of Eden, and the very first thing God said was, "It is not good for man to be alone." (Genesis 2:18, NLT). God desires you to be a part of His family.

The gospel's good news is that God has a family, and we're invited to join it through faith in Jesus.

> "Even before he made the world, God loved us and chose us in Christ to be holy and without fault in his eyes. God decided in advance to adopt us into his own family by bringing us to himself through Jesus Christ. This is what he

wanted to do, and it gave him great pleasure. So we praise God for the glorious grace he has poured out on us who belong to his dear Son." –Ephesians 1:4-6 (NLT)

Is our family only about biology? No, it's more than that. When we accept Jesus as our Lord and Savior, we become part of two families. We have our biological family with parents and siblings, and we're also adopted into God's family.

"For his Spirit joins with our spirit to affirm that we are God's children." –Romans 8:16 (NLT)

Some Christians are part of three families: biological, adopted, and God's family. Imagine a place without families, where the government raises children. In such a place, it's hard to understand our close relationship with God as His children. When God saves us, it's not bureaucratic but a loving Father welcoming us into His family. God gave us families so we can grasp the honor of becoming His beloved sons and daughters.

The parallels are easy to see. When we are born physically, we enter a physical family. However, when we experience a spiritual rebirth or are "born again," we become part of a spiritual family. In Paul's words, we are adopted into God's family.

"So you have not received a spirit that makes you fearful slaves. Instead, you received God's Spirit when he adopted you as his own children. Now we call him, 'Abba, Father.'" –Romans 8:15 (NLT)

"But when the right time came, God sent his Son, born of a woman, subject to the law. God sent him to buy freedom for us who were slaves to the law, so that he could adopt us as his very own children. And because we are his children, God has sent the Spirit of his Son into our hearts, prompting us to call out, 'Abba, Father.' Now you are no longer a slave but God's own child. And since you are his child, God has made you his heir." –Galatians 4:4-7 (NLT)

Within God's spiritual family, which is the Church, God becomes our Father, and Jesus becomes our Brother. This spiritual family is not limited by ethnicity, gender, or social status. As Paul states,

"For you are all children of God through faith in Christ Jesus. And all who have been united with Christ in baptism have put on Christ, like putting on new clothes. There is no longer Jew or Gentile, slave or free, male and female. For you are all one in Christ Jesus. And now that you belong to Christ, you are the true children of Abraham. You are his heirs, and God's promise to Abraham belongs to you." –Galatians 3:26-29

See that promise? It's for you!

Though Jesus Christ is called the only begotten Son of God, believers are described as God's children, born into His family. He GIVES spiritual leaders to teach, encourage, and help us grow and mature in our faith.

"Now these are the GIFTS Christ gave to the church: the apostles, the prophets, the evangelists, and the pastors and teachers. Their responsibility is to equip God's people to do his work and build up the church, the body of Christ. This will continue until we all come to such unity in our faith and knowledge of God's Son that we will be mature in the Lord, measuring up to the full and complete standard of Christ." –Ephesians 4:11-13 (NLT)

The apostle Paul said, "Though I am the least deserving of all God's people, he graciously GAVE me the privilege of telling the Gentiles about the endless treasures available to them in Christ."–Ephesians 3:8 (NLT)

Your spiritual family, which is God's family, will endure even beyond your physical family. Physical families change as they grow, move, and eventually pass away. However, God's spiritual family will exist eternally. This spiritual family includes all who believe in the Lord Jesus Christ as their Savior and come from diverse backgrounds.

> "After this I saw a vast crowd, too great to count, from every nation and tribe and people and language, standing in front of the throne and before the Lamb. They were clothed in white robes and held palm branches in their hands." –Revelation 7:9 (NLT)

The key trait of this spiritual family is love for one another, as Jesus commanded:

> "Love each other. Just as I have loved you, you should love each other." –John 13:34 (NLT)

Family shows the relationship between Christ and His Church. Ephesians 5 explains that a husband and wife's connection mirrors Christ's relationship with His followers. In simpler terms, it means that like a husband loves and sacrifices for his wife, Jesus loves His people. And just as a wife responds to her husband's love and follows his guidance, so in the same way the church should respond to Jesus.

Early on, it was evident that family members were meant to care for each other. Family also resembles the church and relationships among Christians. When you're around Christians, you'll frequently hear them call each other "brothers and sisters." This isn't just a casual saying; it signifies the spiritual truth of being part of God's family.

> "Never speak harshly to an older man, but appeal to him respectfully as you would to your own father. Talk to younger men as you would to your own brothers. Treat older women as you would your mother, and treat younger women with all purity as you would your own sisters."
> –1 Timothy 5:1-2 (NLT)

A Family Inheritance

As children of God, what do we inherit? Unlike earthly inheritance received after a parent's passing, believers already experience the rewards of their inheritance by having peace with God through the sacrifice of His Son on the cross.

- **His Kingdom**

> "Then the King will say to those on his right, 'Come, you who are blessed by my Father, inherit the Kingdom prepared for you from the creation of the world." –Matthew 25:34 (NLT)

> "We pleaded with you, encouraged you, and urged you to live your lives in a way that God would consider worthy. For he called you to share in his Kingdom and glory." –1 Thessalonians 2:12 (NLT)

> "Since we are receiving a Kingdom that is unshakable, let us be thankful and please God by worshiping him with holy fear and awe." –Hebrews 12:28 (NLT)

- **Spiritual blessings**

> "All praise to God, the Father of our Lord Jesus Christ, who has blessed us with every spiritual blessing in the heavenly realms because we are united with Christ." –Ephesians 1:3 (NLT)

- **The Holy Spirit**

    "And now you Gentiles have also heard the truth, the Good News that God saves you. And when you believed in Christ, he identified you as his own by giving you the Holy Spirit, whom he promised long ago. The Spirit is God's guarantee that he will GIVE us the inheritance he promised and that he has purchased us to be his own people. He did this so we would praise and glorify him." –Ephesians 1:13-14 (NLT)

- **Eternal salvation**

    "But because Jesus lives forever, his priesthood lasts forever. Therefore he is able, once and forever, to save those who come to God through him. He lives forever to intercede with God on their behalf." –Hebrews 7:24-25 (NLT)

When it feels like everything is falling apart, when you've been hurt or betrayed, you don't need revenge or pity. What you really need is the supernatural support of a community of believers in Jesus Christ. You need the family of God to come around you, to pray, encourage, love, and offer guidance. It's God's GIFT to you!

Your ability to bounce back from life's challenges is closely tied to the people who surround you. I urge you to prioritize your spiritual family. Consider joining a small group Bible study, and stay connected. When tough times come, you'll rely on your spiritual family, and others will rely on you when they face difficulties.

Family is an invaluable GIFT from God. Not only does God promise to GIVE us family, He also promises to GIVE increase which we will discover in the next chapter.

06 | INCREASE

Abundance

Throughout the Bible, we can see that God's nature is one of abundance and growth. Starting in the book of Genesis, we are reminded of His desire to bless us with plentiful harvests and abundant provision. God generously provides rain and sustenance for the earth, ensuring that our physical needs are met.

When we step into the promises He has GIVEN us, we can expect to experience an increase. In the New Testament, Jesus teaches us that God's generosity extends to both the righteous and the unrighteous, as He graciously provides for all.

> "From the dew of heaven and the richness of the earth, may God always GIVE you abundant harvests of grain and bountiful new wine."
> –Genesis 27:28 (NLT)

"He GIVES rain for the earth and water for the fields." –Job 5:10 (NLT)

"When you arrive in the land he swore to GIVE your ancestors, you will have large harvests of grain, new wine, and olive oil, and great herds of cattle, sheep, and goats." –Deuteronomy 7:13b (NLT)

"In that way, you will be acting as true children of your Father in heaven. For he GIVES his sunlight to both the evil and the good, and he sends rain on the just and the unjust alike." –Matthew 5:45 (NLT)

Blessings

God wants to bless us, and He does it generously. We should GIVE as we can, considering what He's GIVEN us. His promise to raise Jesus from the dead and fulfill His blessings to David is a reminder of God's unwavering desire to GIVE us His love and grace.

"All must GIVE as they are able, according to the blessings GIVEN to them by the Lord your God." –Deuteronomy 16:17 (NLT)

"For God had promised to raise him from the dead, not leaving him to rot in the grave. He said, 'I will GIVE you the sacred blessings I promised to David.'" –Acts 13:34 (NLT)

Crown

God promises to exchange our sorrows for joy, turning despair into festive praise. Even in the face of challenges, if we remain faithful, He assures us the crown of life as a reward. What a wonderful reminder of God's intention to bless and reward those who trust and remain steadfast in their faith.

"To all who mourn in Israel, he will GIVE a crown of beauty for ashes, a joyous blessing instead of mourning, festive praise instead of despair. In their righteousness, they will be like great oaks that the Lord has planted for his own glory." –Isaiah 61:3 (NLT)

" . . . But if you remain faithful even when facing death, I will GIVE you the crown of life." –Revelation 2:10 (NLT)

Desires

God's love is clear in His willingness to fulfill our desires when we find joy in Him. He encourages us to follow His will and obey His commands, asking Him to GIVE us the desire to do just that. When we come closer to Him, God GIVES the desires of our hearts, withholding nothing. It's a lovely reminder of His readiness to fulfill our deepest desires when we follow His guidance.

> "Take delight in the Lord, and he will GIVE you your heart's desires." –Psalm 37:4 (NLT)

> "May he GIVE us the desire to do his will in everything and to obey all the commands, decrees, and regulations that he gave our ancestors." –1 Kings 8:58 (NLT)

> "For you have GIVEN him his heart's desire; you have withheld nothing he requested." –Psalm 21:2 (NLT)

Favor

"Now God had GIVEN the chief of staff both respect and affection for Daniel." –Daniel 1:9 (NLT)

Honor

"Then the Lord will be your delight. I will GIVE you great honor and satisfy you with the inheritance I promised to your ancestor Jacob. I, the Lord, have spoken!" –Isaiah 58:14 (NLT)

Keys

Jesus GIVES His followers the keys to the Kingdom of Heaven, granting them authority to make decisions that impact both earth and heaven.

"And I will GIVE you the keys of the Kingdom of Heaven. Whatever you forbid on earth will be forbidden in heaven, and whatever you permit on earth will be permitted in heaven." –Matthew 16:19 (NLT)

Kingdom

Only God, as the ultimate authority, has the power to GIVE or take away kingdoms.

> "I'm going to take Saul's kingdom and GIVE it to David. I will establish the throne of David over Israel as well as Judah, all the way from Dan in the north to Beersheba in the south." –2 Samuel 3:10 (NLT)

> "This is what King Cyrus of Persia says: 'The Lord, the God of heaven, has GIVEN me all the kingdoms of the earth. He has appointed me to build him a Temple at Jerusalem, which is in Judah.'" –Ezra 1:2 (NLT)

> "The Lord has done just as he said he would. He has torn the kingdom from you and GIVEN it to your rival, David." –1 Samuel 28:17 (NLT)

> "Then God will GIVE you a grand entrance into the eternal Kingdom of our Lord and Savior Jesus Christ." –2 Peter 1:11 (NLT)

Name

These verses illustrate how God blesses us with a new name, a name of honor and distinction that surpasses any title GIVEN by others. It's a name that will endure forever, and it signifies His favor and restoration in our lives.

> "I will GIVE them—within the walls of my house— a memorial and a name far greater than sons and daughters could GIVE. For the name I GIVE them is an everlasting one. It will never disappear!" –Isaiah 56:5 (NLT)

> "The nations will see your righteousness. World leaders will be blinded by your glory. And you will be GIVEN a new name by the Lord's own mouth." –Isaiah 62:2 (NLT)

> "On that day I will gather you together and bring you home again. I will GIVE you a good name, a name of distinction, among all the nations of the earth, as I restore your fortunes before their very eyes. I, the Lord, have spoken!" –Zephaniah 3:20 (NLT)

Power

God, who has ultimate power, GIVES us strength and authority. He equips us for success and supports His chosen ones. Everything, including wealth, honor, and strength, comes from God, and He can make people great as He sees fit. God helps the weak and empowers leaders with the resources they need.

> "Remember the Lord your God. He is the one who GIVES you power to be successful, in order to fulfill the covenant he confirmed to your ancestors with an oath." –Deuteronomy 8:18 (NLT)

> "Those who fight against the Lord will be shattered. He thunders against them from heaven; the Lord judges throughout the earth. He GIVES power to his king; he increases the strength of his anointed one." –1 Samuel 2:10 (NLT)

> "Wealth and honor come from you alone, for you rule over everything. Power and might are in your hand, and at your discretion people are made great and GIVEN strength." –1 Chronicles 29:12 (NLT)

"God is awesome in his sanctuary. The God of Israel GIVES power and strength to his people. Praise be to God!" –Psalm 68:35 (NLT)

"He GIVES power to the weak and strength to the powerless." –Isaiah 40:29 (NLT)

"Your Majesty, you are the greatest of kings. The God of heaven has GIVEN you sovereignty, power, strength, and honor." –Daniel 2:37 (NLT)

Prosperity

God wants His people to thrive and prosper. He cares for the poor and protects those in need, offering them prosperity. God protects His people and ensures their well-being and rescue from adversity. He heals wounds, restores peace, and provides beyond expectations. God's provision brings joy and celebration among His people. For those who honor Him, a wonderful inheritance is reserved. God encourages generosity towards the less fortunate, promising blessings in return.

"The Lord will GIVE you prosperity in the land he swore to your ancestors to GIVE you, blessing you with many children, numerous livestock, and abundant crops." –Deuteronomy 28:11 (NLT)

"He GIVES prosperity to the poor and protects those who suffer." –Job 5:11 (NLT)

"The Lord protects them and keeps them alive. He GIVES them prosperity in the land and rescues them from their enemies." –Psalm 41:2 (NLT)

"Nevertheless, the time will come when I will heal Jerusalem's wounds and GIVE it prosperity and true peace." –Jeremiah 33:6 (NLT)

"Amaziah asked the man of God, 'But what about all that silver I paid to hire the army of Israel?' The man of God replied, 'The Lord is able to GIVE you much more than this!'" –2 Chronicles 25:9 (NLT)

"Many sacrifices were offered on that joyous day, for God had GIVEN the people cause for great joy. The women and children also participated in the celebration, and the joy of the people of Jerusalem could be heard far away." –Nehemiah 12:43 (NLT)

"For you have heard my vows, O God. You have GIVEN me an inheritance reserved for those who fear your name." –Psalm 61:5 (NLT)

"The land you have GIVEN me is a pleasant land. What a wonderful inheritance!" –Psalm 16:6 (NLT)

"GIVE generously to the poor, not grudgingly, for the Lord your God will bless you in everything you do." –Deuteronomy 15:10 (NLT)

"GIVE him a generous farewell GIFT from your flock, your threshing floor, and your winepress. Share with him some of the bounty with which the Lord your God has blessed you." –Deuteronomy 15:14 (NLT)

"But you may keep for yourselves all the women, children, livestock, and other plunder. You may enjoy the plunder from your enemies that the Lord your God has GIVEN you." –Deuteronomy 20:14 (NLT)

Reward

God wants His children to succeed, and He rewards them for their faithfulness. He examines hearts and actions, giving each person the rewards they deserve. Even when faced with opportunities for revenge, God's people are encouraged to choose mercy, trusting in His rewards. As believers serve Him faithfully, they are reminded of the inheritance God has prepared for them, secured by His grace. The Holy Spirit serves as a guarantee of this promised inheritance.

"She named him Zebulun, for she said, 'God has GIVEN me a good reward. Now my husband will treat me with respect, for I have GIVEN him six sons." –Genesis 30:20 (NLT)

"But I, the Lord, search all hearts and examine secret motives. I GIVE all people their due rewards, according to what their actions deserve." –Jeremiah 17:10 (NLT)

"The Lord GIVES his own reward for doing good and for being loyal, and I refused to kill you even when the Lord placed you in my power, for you are the Lord's anointed one." –1 Samuel 26:23 (NLT)

"Remember that the Lord will GIVE you an inheritance as your reward, and that the Master you are serving is Christ." –Colossians 3:24 (NLT)

"And now I entrust you to God and the message of his grace that is able to build you up and GIVE you an inheritance with all those he has set apart for himself." –Acts 20:32 (NLT)

"The Spirit is God's guarantee that he will GIVE us the inheritance he promised and that he has purchased us to be his own people. He did this so we would praise and glorify him." –Ephesians 1:14 (NLT)

Success

"'O Lord, God of my master, Abraham,' he prayed. 'Please GIVE me success today, and show unfailing love to my master, Abraham.'" –Genesis 24:12 (NLT)

"So today when I came to the spring, I prayed this prayer: 'O Lord, God of my master, Abraham, please GIVE me success on this mission.'" –Genesis 24:42 (NLT)

"For seven days you must celebrate this festival to honor the Lord your God at the place he chooses, for it is he who blesses you with bountiful harvests and GIVES you success in all your work. This festival will be a time of great joy for all." –Deuteronomy 16:15 (NLT)

"The Lord your God will then make you successful in everything you do. He will GIVE you many children and numerous livestock, and he will cause your fields to produce abundant harvests, for the Lord will again delight in being good to you as he was to your ancestors." –Deuteronomy 30:9 (NLT)

"Now, my son, may the Lord be with you and GIVE you success as you follow his directions in building the Temple of the Lord your God." –1 Chronicles 22:11 (NLT)

"Please, Lord, please save us. Please, Lord, please GIVE us success." –Psalm 118:25 (NLT)

Treasures

> "And I will GIVE you treasures hidden in the darkness—secret riches. I will do this so you may know that I am the Lord, the God of Israel, the one who calls you by name." –Isaiah 45:3 (NLT)

Victory

God passionately desires to GIVE victory to His people. Throughout the Bible, we see how God provided victory in battles and challenges. He empowered individuals and nations, ensuring their success against enemies. Whether it was the strength GIVEN to Joshua, the courage instilled in Gideon, or the support for kings and leaders, God's hand was evident in victories large and small.

Even in spiritual battles, through Jesus Christ, God GIVES us victory over sin and death, offering us hope and assurance.

> "The Lord is my strength and my song; he has GIVEN me victory. This is my God, and I will praise him—my father's God, and I will exalt him!" –Exodus 15:2 (NLT)

"For the Lord your God is going with you! He will fight for you against your enemies, and he will GIVE you victory!" –Deuteronomy 20:4 (NLT)

"But the Lord told me, 'Do not be afraid of him, for I have GIVEN you victory over Og and his entire army, and I will GIVE you all his land. Treat him just as you treated King Sihon of the Amorites, who ruled in Heshbon.'" –Deuteronomy 3:2 (NLT)

"Then the Lord said to Joshua, 'Do not be afraid or discouraged. Take all your fighting men and attack Ai, for I have GIVEN you the king of Ai, his people, his town, and his land.'" –Joshua 8:1 (NLT)

"'Do not be afraid of them,' the Lord said to Joshua, 'for I have GIVEN you victory over them. Not a single one of them will be able to stand up to you.'" –Joshua 10:8 (NLT)

"The rest of you continue chasing the enemy and cut them down from the rear. Don't GIVE them a chance to get back to their towns, for the

Lord your God has GIVEN you victory over them." –Joshua 10:19 (NLT)

"The Lord answered, 'Judah, for I have GIVEN them victory over the land.'" –Judges 1:2 (NLT)

"'Follow me,' he said, 'for the Lord has GIVEN you victory over Moab your enemy.' So they followed him." –Judges 3:28 (NLT)

"Then Deborah said to Barak, 'Get ready! This is the day the Lord will GIVE you victory over Sisera, for the Lord is marching ahead of you.' So Barak led his 10,000 warriors down the slopes of Mount Tabor into battle." –Judges 4:14 (NLT)

"The Lord told Gideon, 'With these 300 men I will rescue you and GIVE you victory over the Midianites. Send all the others home.'" –Judges 7:7 (NLT)

"That night the Lord said, 'Get up! Go down into the Midianite camp, for I have GIVEN you victory over them!'" –Judges 7:9 (NLT)

"His companion answered, 'Your dream can mean only one thing—God has GIVEN Gideon son of Joash, the Israelite, victory over Midian and all its allies!'" –Judges 7:14 (NLT)

"When Gideon heard the dream and its interpretation, he bowed in worship before the Lord. Then he returned to the Israelite camp and shouted, 'Get up! For the Lord has GIVEN you victory over the Midianite hordes!'" –Judges 7:15 (NLT)

"So Gideon said, 'After the Lord GIVES me victory over Zebah and Zalmunna, I will return and tear your flesh with the thorns and briers from the wilderness.'" –Judges 8:7 (NLT)

"You have GIVEN me your shield of victory; your help has made me great." –2 Samuel 22:36 (NLT)

"You GIVE great victories to your king; you show unfailing love to your anointed, to David and all his descendants forever." –2 Samuel 22:51 (NLT)

"Then all the men returned to Jerusalem, with Jehoshaphat leading them, overjoyed that the Lord had GIVEN them victory over their enemies." –2 Chronicles 20:27 (NLT)

"You have GIVEN me your shield of victory. Your right hand supports me; your help has made me great." –Psalm 18:35 (NLT)

"You GIVE great victories to your king; you show unfailing love to your anointed, to David and all his descendants forever." –Psalm 18:50 (NLT)

"How the king rejoices in your strength, O Lord! He shouts with joy because you GIVE him victory." –Psalm 21:1 (NLT)

"Lift up your spear and javelin against those who pursue me. Let me hear you say, 'I will GIVE you victory!'" –Psalm 35:33 (NLT)

"You are the one who GIVES us victory over our enemies; you disgrace those who hate us." –Psalm 44:7 (NLT)

"The Lord is my strength and my song; he has GIVEN me victory." –Psalm 118:14 (NLT)

"See, God has come to save me. I will trust in him and not be afraid. The Lord God is my strength and my song; he has GIVEN me victory." –Isaiah 12:2 (NLT)

" . . . I will GIVE him victory over kings and princes. He will trample them as a potter treads on clay." –Isaiah 41:25 (NLT)

"The Lord will GIVE victory to the rest of Judah first, before Jerusalem, so that the people of Jerusalem and the royal line of David will not have greater honor than the rest of Judah." –Zechariah 12:7 (NLT)

"But thank God! He GIVES us victory over sin and death through our Lord Jesus Christ." –1 Corinthians 15:57 (NLT)

Wealth

God's desire is to provide the wealth His children need. As seen throughout the Bible, God blessed individuals with flocks, herds, silver, gold, and servants, showering them with prosperity. This wealth was a testament to His faithfulness and His commitment to fulfilling His promises. In Ezekiel, God's covenant of peace signified not only the GIFT of land but also the assurance of abundance and growth.

> "And the Lord has greatly blessed my master; he has become a wealthy man. The Lord has

GIVEN him flocks of sheep and goats, herds of cattle, a fortune in silver and gold, and many male and female servants and camels and donkeys." –Genesis 24:35 (NLT)

"All the wealth God has GIVEN you from our father legally belongs to us and our children. So go ahead and do whatever God has told you." –Genesis 31:16 (NLT)

"He built many towns and acquired vast flocks and herds, for God had GIVEN him great wealth." –2 Chronicles 32:29 (NLT)

"And I will make a covenant of peace with them, an everlasting covenant. I will GIVE them their land and increase their numbers, and I will put my Temple among them forever." –Ezekiel 37:26 (NLT)

Many Christians argue over God's promises to GIVE increase. Flip back through this chapter and decide which verses you want to rip out of your Bible. An honest study of the Scriptures offers only one conclusion: God promises to GIVE increase. Don't allow anyone to rob you of any of God's promises to GIVE. Allow the whole Word of God to speak!

Keep in mind, God's "more" is always more of Him and more for Him. This includes God's promise to GIVE increase. Regardless of whether or not He actually puts the increase in your hands - it's all for Him. The more you experience God as the GIVER the more you will conclude Jesus is worthy of everything God promises to increase. Now, receive the GIFTS of God.

In the next chapter, we will see all the scriptures in the Bible where God promises to GIVE His empowerment to us.

07 | EMPOWERMENT

God's GIFTS are crucial for guiding and empowering His children to follow His divine will and purpose. Through these provisions, God equips and supports His people on their spiritual journey with the necessary tools and guidance.

Ability

God generously GIVES His children special abilities and skills through His Spirit. Some receive the GIFT of wise advice, while others gain special knowledge. Although love should be our top priority, we are encouraged to desire spiritual GIFTS, particularly the ability to prophesy. God wants us to seek and use these abilities to strengthen the entire church community.

> "To one person the Spirit GIVES the ability to GIVE wise advice; to another the same Spirit GIVES a message of special knowledge."
> –1 Corinthians 12:8 (NLT)

> "Let love be your highest goal! But you should also desire the special abilities the Spirit GIVES—especially the ability to prophesy."
> –1 Corinthians 14:1 (NLT)

> "And the same is true for you. Since you are so eager to have the special abilities the Spirit GIVES, seek those that will strengthen the whole church." –1 Corinthians 14:12 (NLT)

Decrees

Decrees are like official rules from God. They are the specific laws and commands that God gave to the Israelites through Moses. It's important to obediently follow all these divine instructions GIVEN by God.

> "And you must teach the Israelites all the decrees that the Lord has GIVEN them through Moses." –Leviticus 10:11 (NLT)

> "You must diligently obey the commands of the Lord your God—all the laws and decrees he has GIVEN you." –Deuteronomy 6:17 (NLT)

Choice

God GIVES us the GIFT of free will. We have the choice between life and death, blessings and curses. God wants us to choose life for ourselves and future generations. To do this, we should love and obey the Lord, continually committing ourselves to Him. This choice leads to a meaningful life and highlights God's enduring care for us.

> "Today I have GIVEN you the choice between life and death, between blessings and curses. Now I call on heaven and earth to witness the choice you make. Oh, that you would choose life, so that you and your descendants might live!" –Deuteronomy 30:19 (NLT)

> "You can make this choice by loving the Lord your God, obeying him, and committing yourself firmly to him. This is the key to your life. And if you love and obey the Lord, you will live long in the land the Lord swore to GIVE your ancestors Abraham, Isaac, and Jacob." –Deuteronomy 30:20 (NLT)

Comfort

God comforts us in our troubles so we can comfort others. As we face difficulties, we receive His comforting grace. This empowers us to offer the same comfort to those who are going through tough times.

> "He comforts us in all our troubles so that we can comfort others. When they are troubled, we will be able to GIVE them the same comfort God has GIVEN us." –2 Corinthians 1:4 (NLT)

> "We are confident that as you share in our sufferings, you will also share in the comfort God GIVES us." –2 Corinthians 1:7 (NLT)

Commands

God's commands are for our good. When we obey them, we're seen as righteous by the Lord. Be careful not to change them. They remind us of our freedom from slavery to sin. Just as Joshua followed these commands, we should too, knowing they're for our benefit.

> "For we will be counted as righteous when we obey all the commands the Lord our God has GIVEN us." –Deuteronomy 6:25 (NLT)

"So be careful to obey all the commands I GIVE you. You must not add anything to them or subtract anything from them." –Deuteronomy 12:32 (NLT)

"Always remember that you were slaves in Egypt and that the Lord your God redeemed you from your slavery. That is why I have GIVEN you this command." –Deuteronomy 24:18 (NLT)

"As the Lord had commanded his servant Moses, so Moses commanded Joshua. And Joshua did as he was told, carefully obeying all the commands that the Lord had GIVEN to Moses." –Joshua 11:15 (NLT)

Holiness

Holiness is a GIFT from God that shapes our sincerity and integrity. It means being morally and spiritually pure, or set apart for a sacred purpose.

"We can say with confidence and a clear conscience that we have lived with a God-GIVEN holiness and sincerity in all our dealings." –2 Corinthians 1:12 (NLT)

Holy Spirit

God freely GIVES us His Holy Spirit, a promised GIFT. When we ask, Jesus assures us that our heavenly Father readily GIVES His Spirit. He speaks God's words limitlessly and fills our hearts with love. The Spirit acts as a guarantee, confirming our connection with God.

> "And I will ask the Father, and he will GIVE you another Advocate, who will never leave you."
> –John 14:16 (NLT)

> " . . . how much more will your heavenly Father GIVE the Holy Spirit to those who ask him."
> –Luke 11:13 (NLT)

> "For he is sent by God. He speaks God's words, for God GIVES him the Spirit without limit."
> –John 3:34 (NLT)

> "And this hope will not lead to disappointment. For we know how dearly God loves us, because he has GIVEN us the Holy Spirit to fill our hearts with his love." –Romans 5:5 (NLT)

> "God himself has prepared us for this, and as a guarantee he has GIVEN us his Holy Spirit."
> –2 Corinthians 5:5 (NLT)

"But you are not like that, for the Holy One has GIVEN you his Spirit, and all of you know the truth." –1 John 2:20 (NLT)

"And God has GIVEN us his Spirit as proof that we live in him and he in us." –1 John 4:13 (NLT)

Instructions

God provides us with important instructions for our well-being and guidance. Moses received these teachings from the Lord and shared them with the people of Israel, who committed to following them. These instructions serve as a lasting reminder and a covenant with God. They provide wisdom, direction, and a satisfying life in alignment with God's purpose.

"Then Moses climbed the mountain to appear before God. The Lord called to him from the mountain and said, "GIVE these instructions to the family of Jacob; announce it to the descendants of Israel." –Exodus 19:3 (NLT)

"Then all the people of Israel approached him, and Moses GAVE them all the instructions

the Lord had GIVEN him on Mount Sinai."
–Exodus 34:32 (NLT)

"Then Moses went down to the people and repeated all the instructions and regulations the Lord had GIVEN him. All the people answered with one voice, 'We will do everything the Lord has commanded.'" –Exodus 24:3 (NLT)

"Then the Lord said to Moses, 'Come up to me on the mountain. Stay there, and I will GIVE you the tablets of stone on which I have inscribed the instructions and commands so you can teach the people.'" –Exodus 24:12 (NLT)

"The Lord GIVES the word, and a great army brings the good news." –Psalm 68:11 (NLT)

"'And this is my covenant with them,' says the Lord. 'My Spirit will not leave them, and neither will these words I have GIVEN you. They will be on your lips and on the lips of your children and your children's children forever. I, the Lord, have spoken!'" –Isaiah 59:21 (NLT)

Knowledge

God generously GIVES us knowledge, providing a guide to lead us with wisdom and understanding. When we please Him, He blesses us with wisdom and joy. His law offers us complete knowledge and truth, and even when we make our own plans, the Lord GIVES us the right answers.

> "And I will GIVE you shepherds after my own heart, who will guide you with knowledge and understanding." –Jeremiah 3:15 (NLT)

> "God GIVES wisdom, knowledge, and joy to those who please him. But if a sinner becomes wealthy, God takes the wealth away and GIVES it to those who please him. This, too, is meaningless—like chasing the wind." –Ecclesiastes 2:26 (NLT)

> " . . . For you are certain that God's law GIVES you complete knowledge and truth." –Romans 2:20 (NLT)

> "We can make our own plans, but the Lord GIVES the right answer." –Proverbs 16:1 (NLT)

Legal requirement

Eleazar, the high priest, told the Israelite soldiers to purify the spoils of war that could withstand fire. This cleansing likely represented removing impurities from the enemy's possessions. In Numbers 31, the Israelites carried out God's command to punish the Midianites for leading them astray. God's GIFT of requirements served to protect His people.

> "Then Eleazar the priest said to the men who were in the battle, 'The Lord has GIVEN Moses this legal requirement . . . " –Numbers 31:21 (NLT)

Light

God's Word is a guiding light for all, and Jesus, the true Light, came into the world to enlighten everyone. God's truth is accessible to those who seek it. It offers clarity and illumination on our spiritual journey.

> "The teaching of your word GIVES light, so even the simple can understand." –Psalm 119:130 (NLT)

"The one who is the true light, who GIVES light to everyone, was coming into the world."
–John 1:9 (NLT)

Message

God shares His message with His people, urging them to be holy and share it with others. While in prison, Jeremiah received messages from God, even concerning foreign nations. This illustrates God's commitment to humanity to GIVE His guidance and purpose through chosen messengers.

> "'And you will be my kingdom of priests, my holy nation.' This is the message you must GIVE to the people of Israel." –Exodus 19:6 (NLT)

> "The Lord had GIVEN the following message to Jeremiah while he was still in prison . . . " –Jeremiah 39:15 (NLT)

> "The following messages were GIVEN to Jeremiah the prophet from the Lord concerning foreign nations." –Jeremiah 46:1 (NLT)

Plan

> "'Every part of this plan,' David told Solomon, 'was GIVEN to me in writing from the hand of the Lord.'" –1 Chronicles 28:19 (NLT)

Promises

God faithfully keeps His promises. Over time, God fulfilled every promise, leaving none unmet. These promises are a free GIFT received through faith. God's Word is unchanging because He cannot lie. This unshakable assurance in God's promises GIVES us great confidence and hope as we seek refuge in Him. Through His glory and excellence, God generously shares precious promises with us, demonstrating His steadfast commitment to His people.

> "One day Moses said to his brother-in-law, Hobab son of Reuel the Midianite, 'We are on our way to the place the Lord promised us, for he said, "I will GIVE it to you." Come with us and we will treat you well, for the Lord has promised wonderful blessings for Israel!'" –Numbers 10:29 (NLT)

"Not a single one of all the good promises the Lord had GIVEN to the family of Israel was left unfulfilled; everything he had spoken came true." –Joshua 21:45 (NLT)

"So the promise is received by faith. It is GIVEN as a free GIFT. And we are all certain to receive it, whether or not we live according to the law of Moses, if we have faith like Abraham's. For Abraham is the father of all who believe." –Romans 4:16 (NLT)

"So God has GIVEN both his promise and his oath. These two things are unchangeable because it is impossible for God to lie. Therefore, we who have fled to him for refuge can have great confidence as we hold to the hope that lies before us." –Hebrews 6:18 (NLT)

"And because of his glory and excellence, he has GIVEN us great and precious promises . . . " –2 Peter 1:4 (NLT)

Responsibilities

God GIVES us responsibilities based on our faithfulness. Just as the faithful servant in the parable written below is rewarded with more tasks, Paul and Peter were GIVEN responsibilities by God to spread the gospel to various groups. These examples highlight how God entrusts us with duties that align with our commitment to His work, enabling us to serve His church and share His message with others.

"The master was full of praise. 'Well done, my good and faithful servant. You have been faithful in handling this small amount, so now I will GIVE you many more responsibilities. Let's celebrate together!'" –Matthew 25:21 (NLT)

"Instead, they saw that God had GIVEN me the responsibility of preaching the gospel to the Gentiles, just as he had GIVEN Peter the responsibility of preaching to the Jews." –Galatians 2:7 (NLT)

"God has GIVEN me the responsibility of serving his church by proclaiming his entire message to you." –Colossians 1:25 (NLT)

Shepherds

"And I will GIVE you shepherds after my own heart, who will guide you with knowledge and understanding." –Jeremiah 3:15 (NLT)

Skills

"The Lord has GIVEN them special skills as engravers, designers, embroiderers in blue, purple, and scarlet thread on fine linen cloth, and weavers. They excel as craftsmen and as designers." –Exodus 35:34 (NLT)

Spirit

God only GIVES us good things, not fear or timidity. Instead, He grants us a spirit of power, love, and self-discipline.

"For God has not GIVEN us a spirit of fear and timidity, but of power, love, and self-discipline." –2 Timothy 1:7 (NLT)

Strength

The Lord generously GIVES us strength, serving as our safe place. He also blesses us with peace. When we ask, He provides us with what we need, and shapes and empowers us to fulfill His purposes. Through Christ, we can do all things because He strengthens us.

> "The Lord GIVES his people strength. He is a safe fortress for his anointed king." –Psalm 28:8 (NLT)

> "The Lord GIVES his people strength. The Lord blesses them with peace." –Psalm 29:11 (NLT)

> "Look down and have mercy on me. GIVE your strength to your servant; save me, the son of your servant." –Psalm 86:16 (NLT)

> "And now the Lord speaks—the one who formed me in my mother's womb to be his servant, who commissioned me to bring Israel back to him. The Lord has honored me, and my God has GIVEN me strength." –Isaiah 49:5 (NLT)

> "For I can do everything through Christ, who GIVES me strength." –Philippians 4:13 (NLT)

Task

God's GIFT to us is the important task of reconciling people to Him. Helping people find new life in Christ brings joy like nothing else.

> "And all of this is a GIFT from God, who brought us back to himself through Christ. And God has GIVEN us this task of reconciling people to him." –2 Corinthians 5:18 (NLT)

Understanding

God provides generous understanding through leaders, His commandments, and our openness to listen. He GIVES insight and knowledge, and Jesus, the Son of God, offers understanding to know the true God and have fellowship with Him.

> "And I will GIVE you shepherds after my own heart, who will guide you with knowledge and understanding." –Jeremiah 3:15 (NLT)

"Your commandments GIVE me understanding; no wonder I hate every false way of life." –Psalm 119:104 (NLT)

"The farmer knows just what to do, for God has GIVEN him understanding." –Isaiah 28:26 (NLT)

"He explained to me, 'Daniel, I have come here to GIVE you insight and understanding.'" –Daniel 9:22 (NLT)

"To those who listen to my teaching, more understanding will be GIVEN, and they will have an abundance of knowledge." –Matthew 13:12 (NLT)

"Then he added, 'Pay close attention to what you hear. The closer you listen, the more understanding you will be GIVEN—and you will receive even more.'" –Mark 4:24 (NLT)

"To those who listen to my teaching, more understanding will be GIVEN." –Mark 4:25 (NLT)

"So pay attention to how you hear. To those who listen to my teaching, more understanding will be GIVEN." –Luke 8:18 (NLT)

"And we know that the Son of God has come, and he has GIVEN us understanding so that we can know the true God. And now we live in fellowship with the true God because we live in fellowship with his Son, Jesus Christ. He is the only true God, and he is eternal life." –1 John 5:20 (NLT)

Warning

God's warnings are valuable GIFTS, and we are instructed to take them to heart, passing them on to the next generation for their benefit and obedience.

"He added: 'Take to heart all the words of warning I have GIVEN you today. Pass them on as a command to your children so they will obey every word of these instructions.'" –Deuteronomy 32:46 (NLT)

Wisdom

God generously GIVES wisdom to those who seek it. We can ask Him for wisdom without hesitation. Throughout history, individuals like King Solomon received extraordinary wisdom from God, making just decisions and providing comfort to others. The Lord imparts wisdom to those who seek it, influencing world events and aiding scholars. God's wisdom is a valuable GIFT, and we can ask for it with confidence.

"If you need wisdom, ask our generous God, and he will GIVE it to you. He will not rebuke you for asking." –James 1:5 (NLT)

"When all Israel heard the king's decision, the people were in awe of the king, for they saw the wisdom God had GIVEN him for rendering justice." –1 Kings 3:28 (NLT)

"People from every nation came to consult him and to hear the wisdom God had GIVEN him." –1 Kings 10:24 (NLT)

"And may the Lord GIVE you wisdom and understanding, that you may obey the Law of the Lord your God as you rule over Israel." –1 Chronicles 22:12 (NLT)

"And you, Ezra, are to use the wisdom your God has GIVEN you to appoint magistrates and judges who know your God's laws to govern all the people in the province west of the Euphrates River." –Ezra 7:25 (NLT)

"The Lord of Heaven's Armies is a wonderful teacher, and he GIVES the farmer great wisdom." –Isaiah 28:29 (NLT)

"The Sovereign Lord has GIVEN me his words of wisdom, so that I know how to comfort the weary. Morning by morning he wakens me and opens my understanding to his will." –Isaiah 50:4 (NLT)

"He controls the course of world events; he removes kings and sets up other kings. He GIVES wisdom to the wise and knowledge to the scholars." –Daniel 2:21 (NLT)

"I thank and praise you, God of my ancestors, for you have GIVEN me wisdom and strength. You have told me what we asked of you and revealed to us what the king demanded." –Daniel 2:23 (NLT)

> "But the Lord in his mercy has GIVEN me wisdom that can be trusted, and I will share it with you." –1 Corinthians 7:25 (NLT)

Empowerment is a priceless GIFT from God. As we consider all the scriptures in the Bible where God promises to GIVE land, life, increase, and empowerment we have no choice but to understand God promises to GIVE us "everything," which we will study in the next chapter.

08 | EVERYTHING

God provides us with everything we have, whether it's material blessings, wisdom, joy, or even His own Son. He doesn't hold back but generously GIVES us what we need. Even things like rain, crops, and food show His goodness. We should trust in God, who abundantly supplies all we need for our enjoyment. Through His divine power, He equips us with everything required for a godly life when we come to know Him. God's GIFTS are a constant reminder of His love and care for us.

> "No one can receive anything unless God GIVES it from heaven." –John 3:27 (NLT)

> "Since he did not spare even his own Son but GAVE him up for us all, won't he also GIVE us everything else?" –Romans 8:32 (NLT)

> "For what GIVES you the right to make such a judgment? What do you have that God hasn't GIVEN you? And if everything you have is from God, why boast as though it were not a GIFT?" –1 Corinthians 4:7 (NLT)

"'And I have GIVEN every green plant as food for all the wild animals, the birds in the sky, and the small animals that scurry along the ground—everything that has life.' And that is what happened." –Genesis 1:30 (NLT)

"And this memorial pillar I have set up will become a place for worshiping God, and I will present to God a tenth of everything he GIVES me." –Genesis 28:22 (NLT)

"I will certainly GIVE you the wisdom and knowledge you requested. But I will also GIVE you wealth, riches, and fame such as no other king has had before you or will ever have in the future!" –2 Chronicles 1:12 (NLT)

"You have GIVEN me greater joy than those who have abundant harvests of grain and new wine." –Psalm 4:7 (NLT)

"But GIVE great joy to those who came to my defense. Let them continually say, 'Great is the Lord, who delights in blessing his servant with peace!'" –Psalm 35:27 (NLT)

"You have endowed him with eternal blessings and GIVEN him the joy of your presence." –Psalm 21:6 (NLT)

"Oh, GIVE me back my joy again; you have broken me—now let me rejoice." –Psalm 51:8 (NLT)

"God places the lonely in families; he sets the prisoners free and GIVES them joy." –Psalm 68:6 (NLT)

"GIVE us gladness in proportion to our former misery! Replace the evil years with good." –Psalm 90:15 (NLT)

"God GIVES some people great wealth and honor and everything they could ever want, but then he doesn't GIVE them the chance to enjoy these things. They die, and someone else, even a stranger, ends up enjoying their wealth! This is meaningless—a sickening tragedy." –Ecclesiastes 6:2 (NLT)

"Restore us, O Lord, and bring us back to you again! GIVE us back the joys we once had!" –Lamentations 5:21 (NLT)

"GIVE me happiness, O Lord, for I GIVE myself to you." –Psalm 86:4 (NLT)

"I will cleanse you of your filthy behavior. I will GIVE you good crops of grain, and I will send no more famines on the land." –Ezekiel 36:29 (NLT)

We are to demonstrate God's generosity in our actions.

"In that way, you will be acting as true children of your Father in heaven. For he GIVES his sunlight to both the evil and the good, and he sends rain on the just and the unjust alike." –Matthew 5:45 (NLT)

"I will GIVE you great harvests from your fruit trees and fields, and never again will the surrounding nations be able to scoff at your land for its famines." –Ezekiel 36:30 (NLT)

"The Lord says, 'I will GIVE you back what you lost to the swarming locusts, the hopping locusts, the stripping locusts, and the cutting locusts. It was I who sent this great destroying army against you.'" –Joel 2:25 (NLT)

"Seek the Kingdom of God above all else, and live righteously, and he will GIVE you everything you need." –Matthew 6:33 (NLT)

"Seek the Kingdom of God above all else, and he will GIVE you everything you need." –Luke 12:31 (NLT)

"But he never left them without evidence of himself and his goodness. For instance, he sends you rain and good crops and GIVES you food and joyful hearts." –Acts 14:17 (NLT)

"Since he did not spare even his own Son but GAVE him up for us all, won't he also GIVE us everything else?" –Romans 8:32 (NLT)

"And this same God who takes care of me will supply all your needs from his glorious riches, which have been GIVEN to us in Christ Jesus." –Philippians 4:19 (NLT)

"Their trust should be in God, who richly GIVES us all we need for our enjoyment." –1 Timothy 6:17 (NLT)

"By his divine power, God has GIVEN us everything we need for living a godly life. We have received all of this by coming to know him, the one who called us to himself by means of his marvelous glory and excellence." –2 Peter 1:3 (NLT)

Future

As the sovereign Creator, God firmly controls the future, actively shaping it with His divine plans of goodness and hope. The scriptures reassure us that God's intentions are not to bring disaster but to fulfill future promises. This provides comfort and trust in His guidance, allowing us to anticipate the wonderful things He has prepared for us.

> "'For I know the plans I have for you,' says the Lord. 'They are plans for good and not for disaster, to GIVE you a future and a hope.'" –Jeremiah 29:11 (NLT)

Gifts

God's grace overflows as He generously GIVES us various GIFTS, each with a unique purpose. He encourages us to use these GIFTS with faith. Through Christ, we receive these unique GIFTS, which are meant to support and help one another. The Holy Spirit empowers individuals with different GIFTS, including faith, healing, miracles, prophecy, discernment, speaking in unknown languages, and interpretation. His GIFTS to us are meant to be used rather than placed on a shelf for display, or packed away in a hidden closet.

> "In his grace, God has GIVEN us different GIFTS for doing certain things well. So if God has GIVEN you the ability to prophesy, speak out with as much faith as God has GIVEN you." –Romans 12:6 (NLT)

> "I always thank my God for you and for the gracious GIFTS he has GIVEN you, now that you belong to Christ Jesus." –1 Corinthians 1:4 (NLT)

> "A spiritual GIFT is GIVEN to each of us so we can help each other." –1 Corinthians 12:7 (NLT)

> "The same Spirit GIVES great faith to another, and to someone else the one Spirit GIVES the GIFT of healing." –1 Corinthians 12:9 (NLT)

> "He GIVES one person the power to perform miracles, and another the ability to prophesy.

He GIVES someone else the ability to discern whether a message is from the Spirit of God or from another spirit. Still another person is GIVEN the ability to speak in unknown languages, while another is GIVEN the ability to interpret what is being said." –1 Corinthians 12:10 (NLT)

"However, he has GIVEN each one of us a special GIFT through the generosity of Christ." –Ephesians 4:7 (NLT)

"God has GIVEN each of you a GIFT from his great variety of spiritual GIFTS. Use them well to serve one another." –1 Peter 4:10 (NLT)

Good Things

God's generosity knows no limits, and He showers us with an abundance of good things. We are reminded to celebrate the countless blessings the Lord has GIVEN to us and our families. However, we must also heed the warning that if we disobey Him, we risk losing these good things. Have you witnessed the wonder of God's goodness as He performs miraculous deeds that leave you in awe? God's goodness is a constant reminder of His love and care for us.

"Afterward you may go and celebrate because of all the good things the Lord your God has GIVEN to you and your household." –Deuteronomy 26:11 (NLT)

"But as surely as the Lord your God has GIVEN you the good things he promised, he will also bring disaster on you if you disobey him. He will completely destroy you from this good land he has GIVEN you." –Joshua 23:15 (NLT)

"They were completely amazed and said again and again, 'Everything he does is wonderful. He even makes the deaf to hear and GIVES speech to those who cannot speak.'" –Mark 7:37 (NLT)

Justice

God's generous nature is evident in the way He consistently GIVES justice to His people, especially when they find themselves weak and oppressed. We pray for His justice day and night, knowing He hears our plea. His justice is marked by fairness and compassion, delivering the oppressed and providing for the needy. God's justice is a source of hope and courage for those who seek it.

"Indeed, the Lord will GIVE justice to his people, and he will change his mind about his servants, when he sees their strength is gone and no one is left, slave or free." –Deuteronomy 32:36 (NLT)

"And may these words that I have prayed in the presence of the Lord be before him constantly, day and night, so that the Lord our God may GIVE justice to me and to his people Israel, according to each day's needs." –1 Kings 8:59 (NLT)

"Would he use his great power to argue with me? No, he would GIVE me a fair hearing." –Job 23:6 (NLT)

"Declare me not guilty, O Lord my God, for you GIVE justice. Don't let my enemies laugh about me in my troubles." –Psalm 35:24 (NLT)

"Pour out your unfailing love on those who love you; GIVE justice to those with honest hearts." –Psalm 36:10 (NLT)

"The Lord GIVES righteousness and justice to all who are treated unfairly." –Psalm 103:6 (NLT)

"For the Lord will GIVE justice to his people and have compassion on his servants." –Psalm 135:14 (NLT)

"But I know the Lord will help those they persecute; he will GIVE justice to the poor." –Psalm 140:12 (NLT)

"He GIVES justice to the oppressed and food to the hungry. The Lord frees the prisoners." –Psalm 146:7 (NLT)

"The poor and the oppressor have this in common—the Lord GIVES sight to the eyes of both." –Proverbs 29:13 (NLT)

"He will GIVE a longing for justice to their judges. He will GIVE great courage to their warriors who stand at the gates." –Isaiah 28:6 (NLT)

"He who GIVES me justice is near. Who will dare to bring charges against me now? Where are my accusers? Let them appear!" –Isaiah 50:8 (NLT)

Love

God invites us to come to Him ready to listen. He promises an everlasting covenant filled with the unfailing love He once pledged to David. This enduring love, GIVEN freely, reminds us of His unchanging affection and faithfulness, available to all who seek refuge in His embrace.

> "Come to me with your ears wide open. Listen, and you will find life. I will make an everlasting covenant with you. I will GIVE you all the unfailing love I promised to David." –Isaiah 55:3 (NLT)

Mercy

Mercy is a compassionate and forgiving act of kindness GIVEN to those in need. Just as God Almighty was asked to grant mercy to Joseph's brothers, our Heavenly Father continually offers us His merciful grace, forgiving our shortcomings, and guiding us through life's trials with compassion and love.

> "May God Almighty GIVE you mercy as you go before the man, so that he will release Simeon

and let Benjamin return." –Genesis 43:14 (NLT)

Ministry

We are encouraged to work diligently in sharing the good news of Jesus and fulfilling the ministries that God has GIVEN to us. Each of us has a unique role and purpose in God's grand plan, and it is our responsibility to embrace and carry out these ministries to make a positive impact on others and spread the message of hope and salvation.

> "Work at telling others the Good News, and fully carry out the ministry God has GIVEN you." –2 Timothy 4:5 (NLT)

Oneness

Before His arrest and crucifixion, Jesus prayed for His disciples, expressing His desire for them to be united just as He and the Father are one. He asked God to GIVE His glory to His disciples so they could work together with a common purpose.

> "I have GIVEN them the glory you GAVE me, so they may be one as we are one." –John 17:22 (NLT)

Patience

God generously GIVES us patience and encouragement, allowing us to live in harmony with others, following the teachings of Christ Jesus.

> "May God, who GIVES this patience and encouragement, help you live in complete harmony with each other, as is fitting for followers of Christ Jesus." –Romans 15:5 (NLT)

Peace

God, as the supreme source of peace, offers a GIFT that goes far beyond anything the world can provide. Jesus GIVES us the invaluable GIFT of peace for our hearts and minds, providing reassurance against fear and anxiety. This peace not only includes liberation from fear, but also security in our territories, and friendly connections with others. It flows as a river of prosperity, serves as a place of refuge for His followers, and remains a constant presence in our daily lives.

> "I am leaving you with a GIFT—peace of mind and heart. And the peace I GIVE is a GIFT the world cannot GIVE. So don't be troubled or afraid." –John 14:27 (NLT)

> "I will GIVE you peace in the land, and you will be able to sleep with no cause for fear. I will rid the land of wild animals and keep your enemies out of your land." –Leviticus 26:6 (NLT)

> "May the Lord show you his favor and GIVE you his peace." –Numbers 6:26 (NLT)

> "But now the Lord my God has GIVEN me peace on every side; I have no enemies, and all is well." –1 Kings 5:4 (NLT)

> "'The Lord your God is with you,' he declared. 'He has GIVEN you peace with the surrounding nations. He has handed them over to me, and they are now subject to the Lord and his people.'" –1 Chronicles 22:18 (NLT)

"For David said, 'The Lord, the God of Israel, has GIVEN us peace, and he will always live in Jerusalem.'" –1 Chronicles 23:25 (NLT)

"This is what the Lord says: 'I will GIVE Jerusalem a river of peace and prosperity. The wealth of the nations will flow to her. Her children will be nursed at her breasts, carried in her arms, and held on her lap.'" –Isaiah 66:12 (NLT)

"I myself will tend my sheep and GIVE them a place to lie down in peace, says the Sovereign Lord." –Ezekiel 34:15 (NLT)

"And now may God, who GIVES us his peace, be with you all. Amen." –Romans 15:33 (NLT)

"Now may the Lord of peace himself GIVE you his peace at all times and in every situation. The Lord be with you all." –2 Thessalonians 3:16 (NLT)

Right standing

God's grace is a profound GIFT that transforms our relationship with Him. He carefully selects us and invites us into His presence, granting us right standing with Him. This divine favor eliminates any accusations against us, for God Himself has provided us with this righteous status.

> "And having chosen them, he called them to come to him. And having called them, he GAVE them right standing with himself. And having GIVEN them right standing, he GAVE them his glory." –Romans 8:30 (NLT)

> "Who dares accuse us whom God has chosen for his own? No one—for God himself has GIVEN us right standing with himself." –Romans 8:33 (NLT)

Right words

In moments of uncertainty and challenge, God provides us with the right words to speak. When faced with difficult situations or persecution, there's no need to worry about our response, for God will GIVE us the appropriate words precisely when we need them. Jesus promises to GIVE us not only the right words, but also profound wisdom that will leave our opponents speechless. The Holy Spirit also imparts words to us, enabling us to communicate spiritual truths with divine guidance.

> "When you are arrested, don't worry about how to respond or what to say. God will GIVE you the right words at the right time." –Matthew 10:19 (NLT)

> "For I will GIVE you the right words and such wisdom that none of your opponents will be able to reply or refute you!" –Luke 21:15 (NLT)

> "When we tell you these things, we do not use words that come from human wisdom. Instead, we speak words GIVEN to us by the Spirit, using the Spirit's words to explain spiritual truths." –1 Corinthians 2:13 (NLT)

Everything means everything. It doesn't mean some things, a few things, or almost everything. It means everything! Do you now accept that? You should. This is the Word of God. He promises to GIVE you everything.

God's promises to GIVE land, life, increase, empowerment, and everything comes with one requirement: Ask, which we will focus on in the next chapter.

09 | ASK

Prayer is how we talk to God about what we need and want. Even though God already knows our needs, prayer is the way God has chosen to answer them. When you pray in your faith journey, it's not just a ritual; it's a life-changing experience. Asking opens the door to God's wisdom and guidance. It's not about using fancy words; it's about being sincere. When you seek, you'll find, and when you knock, doors of opportunity and understanding will open for you.

> "Keep on asking, and you will receive what you ask for. Keep on seeking, and you will find. Keep on knocking, and the door will be opened to you." –Matthew 7:7 (NLT)

> "And so I tell you, keep on asking, and you will receive what you ask for. Keep on seeking, and you will find. Keep on knocking, and the door will be opened to you." –Luke 11:9 (NLT)

Ask, seek, knock. These three actions have distinct meanings. Asking means using words to request from

God. Seeking goes beyond asking; it means setting priorities and focusing your heart. Knocking involves taking physical action. While asking and seeking are important, knocking completes the process. If you need something from someone behind a door, it's natural to keep knocking until they open the door and fulfill your request. Similarly, as a believer, you should pray in faith for God's help and keep praying persistently.

Jesus is not saying that believers always get what they ask for—wrong motives, for example, will hinder answers to prayer. James 4:3 tells us that in this case we want only what will GIVE us pleasure. The more time we spend in the presence of God, the more we will know what to ask for that fits in with God's will. He does not hide from us.

> "Seek the Kingdom of God above all else, and live righteously, and he will GIVE you everything you need." –Matthew 6:33 (NLT)

Seeking involves staying alert and attentive. Pursuing God's kingdom means prioritizing God's plan, and seeking God's righteousness means focusing on personal holiness and wanting to become more like Him.

Remember that He hears you.

Do you know how much He loves you? Maybe not. His love is too big to comprehend! Over and over in the scriptures, He reminds us of that love, and how valuable you are to Him. He's watching over you, and He's listening for your voice. He loves your prayers because they are conversations with Him.

> "You didn't choose me. I chose you. I appointed you to go and produce lasting fruit, so that the Father will GIVE you whatever you ask for, using my name." –John 15:16 (NLT)

> "And we are confident that he hears us whenever we ask for anything that pleases him. And since we know he hears us when we make our requests, we also know that he will GIVE us what we ask for." –1 John 5:14-15 (NLT)

> "You haven't done this before. Ask, using my name, and you will receive, and you will have abundant joy." –John 16:24 (NLT)

Remember that He is generous.

God showed incredible generosity to King Solomon. Early in his reign, God appeared to the king during the night and asked him a profound question:

> "That night God appeared to Solomon and said, 'What do you want? Ask, and I will GIVE it to you!'" –2 Chronicles 1:7 (NLT)

> "That night the Lord appeared to Solomon in a dream, and God said, 'What do you want? Ask, and I will GIVE it to you!'" –1 Kings 3:5 (NLT)

After Solomon humbly asked God for wisdom to effectively govern the people of Israel, God responded by saying that not only would He grant Solomon wisdom but He would also GIVE him riches and fame, unlike anyone before or after him.

> "And I will also GIVE you what you did not ask for—riches and fame! No other king in all the world will be compared to you for the rest of your life!" –1 Kings 3:13 (NLT)

> "I will GIVE you what you asked for! I will GIVE you a wise and understanding heart such

as no one else has had or ever will have!" –1 Kings 3:12 (NLT)

God loves to show His generosity to those who love Him – to those who ask.

> "So if you sinful people know how to GIVE good GIFTS to your children, how much more will your heavenly Father GIVE good GIFTS to those who ask him." –Matthew 7:11 (NLT)

> "So if you sinful people know how to GIVE good GIFTS to your children, how much more will your heavenly Father GIVE the Holy Spirit to those who ask him." –Luke 11:13 (NLT)

> "You haven't done this before. Ask, using my name, and you will receive, and you will have abundant joy." –John 16:24 (NLT)

> "Jew and Gentile are the same in this respect. They have the same Lord, who GIVES generously to all who call on him." –Romans 10:12 (NLT)

> "Only ask, and I will GIVE you the nations as your inheritance, the whole earth as your possession." –Psalm 2:8 (NLT)

> "Now all glory to God, who is able, through his mighty power at work within us, to accomplish infinitely more than we might ask or think. Glory to him in the church and in Christ Jesus through all generations forever and ever! Amen." –Ephesians 3:20-21 (NLT)

That one phrase in Ephesians 3 stops me in my tracks every time: "God . . . is able, through his mighty power at work within us, to accomplish infinitely more than we might ask or think." Amazing!

Think about Him.

Don't be mistaken. Prayer is not like making a shopping list or writing to Santa Claus. While God does want to answer our prayers and provide for our needs, what He desires most is our love and a meaningful relationship with us.

Focus your attention on Him; on *who* He is and what He can do for you.

> "Search for the Lord and for his strength; continually seek him." –1 Chronicles 16:11 (NLT)

"The one thing I ask of the Lord—the thing I seek most—is to live in the house of the Lord all the days of my life, delighting in the Lord's perfections and meditating in his Temple".
–Psalm 27:4 (NLT)

Make *Him* the central focus of your thoughts. Don't let your problems or your prayer requests fill the picture in your mind. In every worry, every thanksgiving, let your prayers rise.

"Don't worry about anything; instead, pray about everything. Tell God what you need, and thank him for all he has done." –Philippians 4:6 (NLT)

During moments of sincere prayer, you will find both strength and comfort. And when you pray in Jesus' name, anticipate miraculous answers.

"You can ask for anything in my name, and I will do it, so that the Son can bring glory to the Father. Yes, ask me for anything in my name, and I will do it!" –John 14:13-14 (NLT)

"You can pray for anything, and if you have faith, you will receive it." –Matthew 21:22 (NLT)

"But even now I know that God will GIVE you whatever you ask." –John 11:22 (NLT)

"Therefore I tell you, whatever you ask in prayer, believe that you have received it, and it will be yours." –Mark 11:24 (NLT)

"But if you remain in me and my words remain in you, you may ask for anything you want, and it will be granted!" –John 15:7 (NLT)

Seek His wisdom.

Are you struggling with decisions? Ask God for wisdom. He generously provides without judgment, lighting up your path with clarity and peace.

"If you need wisdom, ask our generous God, and he will GIVE it to you. He will not rebuke you for asking. But when you ask him, be sure that your faith is in God alone. Do not waver, for a person with divided loyalty is as unsettled as a wave of the sea that is blown and tossed by the wind." –James 1:5-6 (NLT)

"This is what the Lord says: 'Stop at the crossroads and look around. Ask for the old, godly way, and walk in it. Travel its path, and you will find rest for your souls.'" –Jeremiah 6:16 (NLT)

"Ask me and I will tell you remarkable secrets you do not know about things to come." –Jeremiah 33:3 (NLT)

Are you in a situation where you feel desperate or helpless? David was there many times, and he wrote down his prayers for our encouragement.

"O Lord, hear me as I pray; pay attention to my groaning. Listen to my cry for help, my King and my God, for I pray to no one but you. Listen to my voice in the morning, Lord. Each morning I bring my requests to you and wait expectantly." –Psalm 5:1-3 (NLT)

"From the depths of despair, O Lord, I call for your help. Hear my cry, O Lord. Pay attention to my prayer." –Psalm 130:1-2 (NLT)

"But in my distress I cried out to the Lord; yes, I prayed to my God for help. He heard me from his sanctuary; my cry to him reached his ears." –Psalm 18:6 (NLT)

"Listen closely to my prayer, O Lord; hear my urgent cry. I will call to you whenever I'm in trouble, and you will answer me." –Psalm 86:6-7 (NLT)

"Hear my prayer, O Lord; listen to my plea! Answer me because you are faithful and righteous." –Psalm 143:1 (NLT)

King David learned the secret of asking.

"O Lord, you are so good, so ready to forGIVE, so full of unfailing love for all who ask for your help." –Psalm 86:5 (NLT)

Ask for help.

In early biblical history, we find a testimony of God hearing a woman's desperate cry in the middle of family conflict. Rachel, unable to have children, while her sister Leah had many sons, asked her husband for children. When she remained unable to conceive, she allowed her maidservant Bilhah to marry Jacob so that she could have children through her. It sounds complicated, right? God understands "complicated." He knows all about messy situations in relationships.

> "Rachel named him Dan, for she said, 'God has vindicated me! He has heard my request and GIVEN me a son.'" –Genesis 30:6 (NLT)

Fast forward to another woman who found herself in a similar situation. Hannah was barren, and she deeply desired to have children. As she prayed in the temple, the priest misunderstood her motives and labeled her as intoxicated. But that was not at all the case. The Lord knew. He understood in a way that people could not. And He answered her prayer, giving her a son who would grow up to be a prophet and judge in Israel.

> "Hannah was in deep anguish, crying bitterly as she prayed to the Lord. And she made this vow: 'O Lord of Heaven's Armies, if you will look upon my sorrow and answer my prayer and GIVE me a son, then I will GIVE him back to you. He will be yours for his entire lifetime, and as a sign that he has been dedicated to the Lord, his hair will never be cut.'" –1 Samuel 1:10-11 (NLT)

Be bold.

Knowing that you are in constant need of His help, He has made the offer available to you, and has even provided the Holy Spirit to assist in making your requests.

> "So let us come boldly to the throne of our gracious God. There we will receive his mercy, and we will find grace to help us when we need it most." –Hebrews 4:16 (NLT)

> "Dear friends, if we don't feel guilty, we can come to God with bold confidence. And we will receive from him whatever we ask because we obey him and do the things that please him." –1 John 3:21-22 (NLT)

> " . . . you don't have what you want because you don't ask God for it." –James 4:2 (NLT)

> "Dear friends, if we don't feel guilty, we can come to God with bold confidence. And we will receive from him whatever we ask because we obey him and do the things that please him." –1 John 3:21-22 (NLT)

Jesus Himself understands the power and privilege of "asking." He said, "I will ask the Father, and he will GIVE you another Advocate, who will never leave you." –John 14:16 (NLT)

The Father wants you to ask. Jesus is waiting for you to ask, and the Holy Spirit will help you ask! Your faith moves mountains, your prayers reach heaven, and your voice matters to God. Remember, it's YOU He longs to hear. It's YOUR faith that activates His mighty works. So, ask, seek, knock—and witness how your personal dialogue with God can transform not just your life, but the world around you.

Just ask.

We are to ask and keep on asking. On this side of eternity, we will never graduate from our need to keep asking. The whole point of asking is to depend on God to GIVE His GIFTS. In the next chapter, we will see God's call to DEPEND.

10 | DEPEND

"Depend" means to trust, rely, or lean on someone or something for help or to fulfill a need or expectation. It suggests having confidence that the person or thing you're counting on will come through for you.

Think of all the GIFTS of God described throughout His Word.

Do you really see them?

Do you wish they could be yours?

Do you hope that you might experience some of them . . . someday?

Before we end our time together, may I briefly remind you of some important principles that I've come to depend on?

- **God's Abundant Gifts**

  Throughout the Bible, God emphasizes His generosity in providing for His people. He GIVES us land, rest, salvation, security, and so much more. Understanding and acknowledging these GIFTS is the first step in depending on them.

- **Faith and Obedience**

While God provides these GIFTS, there is often a requirement of faith and obedience attached to them. For instance, in the Land Covenant, God made it clear that the land was a GIFT, but Israel needed to obey His commands to prosper and remain in the land. This shows that dependence on God's GIFTS often involves aligning our lives with His will.

- **Promises Fulfilled**

Many of God's promises are yet to be fully fulfilled, like the complete possession of the Promised Land. This teaches us to be patient and trust God's timing. It's a reminder that God keeps His promises, sometimes quickly, and sometimes over time, but always perfectly according to His divine plan.

- **Life-Changing Discipleship**

Recognizing how important God's GIFTS are in our lives requires a discipleship that transforms us. It's not just about understanding these GIFTS but also putting them into practice in our daily lives. Whether it's resting in God's love, having faith in His salvation, or obeying His will, true discipleship should bring about profound change in us.

- **Asking and Receiving**

When we see the word "ask" connected to God's GIFTS, it emphasizes the importance of seeking God's guidance and provision. Jesus Himself encouraged us to ask, and assured us that we will receive. Depending on God's GIFTS involves actively seeking His help and guidance through prayer.

- **Capitalized Words**

The intentional use of capitalized words like GIFT, GIVE, GIVES, and GIVEN throughout this book highlights how frequently God emphasizes these concepts in His Word. It's a reminder that God's GIFTS are not coincidental but central to our faith and life.

Do you realize that God has GIFTS with your name on them? Depend on the GIFTS of God.

Can you lay aside your feelings of unworthiness and inadequacy? Depend on the GIFTS of God.

Are you anxious to put your hand out in faith and take hold of these GIFTS? Depend on the GIFTS of God.

Will you unwrap the GIFTS by faith, and allow God to place them in your life? Depend on the GIFTS of God.

Will you choose to put the GIFTS to use, and not allow them to stay hidden? Depend on the GIFTS of God.

Will you use them as if your life depends upon them? It does, you know. Depend on the GIFTS of God.

When was the last time you encountered someone living in complete dependence on God's GIFTS? Please list the names of individuals you've heard of or know who live completely reliant on God's GIFTS:

1.

2.

3.

4.

5.

Some may come to mind like George Muller or Mother Teresa, but it's rare to be able to name someone, especially in our modern times.

Allow me to insert my name. Every day my life depends on God's GIFTS. This hasn't always been the case; it didn't happen the day I became a Christ follower. Actually, it was decades later.

As I build Spirit Media, I do so relying entirely on God's GIFTS. I firmly believe that God desires nothing less than for each one of us to embrace a life marked by complete dependence on His GIFTS. Through my personal journey, I've come to understand that living dependent on God's GIFTS honors God, and in return, He honors it!

I pray you will now insert *your* name!

Before we close out this book, I have a very important question for you:

Will you here and now accept God's grace to live by nothing but the hand of God?

Allow God to transition you from earthly bank accounts to His heavenly storerooms and treasuries.

Deny depending on what you can produce and fully depend only on what God can produce.

Will you live solely by the hand of God?

I want to pray over you a prayer I have prayed over millions of people around the world:

I pray your hands will lack no good GIFT from God's hands.

That's GIFTS. It's that easy. Now that's freedom!

Depending on God's GIFTS allows you to live every day as if it's Christmas. The only rightful response to seeing all that God promises to GIVE us in the Bible is to live every day like it is Christmas.

CONCLUSION

CHRISTMAS EVERY DAY

I recall the day when, at the age of thirty, God set me free from the shackles of rejection. Throughout my life, I had tirelessly battled for acceptance. My father, unfortunately, lacked the ability to express his love when I was a child.

I vividly recall the moment when I first experienced the freedom generously GIVEN to me in Christ. I couldn't help but wonder: "So, God desires to offer this to me, unconditionally? I don't need to work for it? I don't have to earn it? This is a free GIFT from God?"

Back then, my perception of God was mostly as a God who was distant and far from being a Father or friend. It's astonishing how, almost three decades later, I've come to intimately know God as both Father and Friend in my everyday experiences.

In my fifth book, "Only God Works," the conclusion was straightforward: *it's the Father who's going to GIVE everything we need.*

Now, with the seventh book titled "GIFTS," I delve deeply into the abundant promises in the Bible where God explicitly declares what He GIVES to us. My life, as well as the foundation of Spirit Media, is built on the unwavering belief in living in reliance on God's gracious GIFTS.

I am convinced that such a life honors God, and in turn, He honors it. Sadly, many Christians never find themselves in a situation where they're compelled to depend entirely on God's GIFTS. With this book, I have aimed to guide you on the path to living a life reliant on the abundant GIFTS God provides.

Many believers fail to embrace the idea that every day is like Christmas. The word Christmas means Christ body. No doubt, Jesus is God's greatest GIFT! Christmas doesn't represent a GIFT God gave us 2,000 years ago, but a GIFT He continues to GIVE us everyday. Jesus isn't a tiny baby in a manger but has been imparted into every believer through the Holy Spirit. Emmanuel means God with us, but some days, we live like God came and then left. We celebrate God's present on Christmas Day but think like He left us the day after Christmas.

No! The truth is, every day is Christmas. Every day is Christ's body. Every day, God is with us. There is no greater GIFT! This GIFT makes all the difference in the world. This is the GIFT of The GIVER that keeps on GIVING. Every day is Christmas.

Typically, people celebrate Christmas by exchanging GIFTS, and children eagerly anticipate receiving presents. Similarly, every child of God should maintain that sense of expectancy every day. I pray that as a result of reading this book, you've come to realize that God showers your life with His GIFTS continuously. Regrettably, the enemy's constant trick is to encourage self-reliance and personal productivity over dependence on God's generous GIFTS.

As you reach the conclusion of this book, you now have opportunity to live each day as if it were Christmas, discovering God's GIFTS in every direction you turn.

Frank truly was one of my GIFTS from God. Even before our paths crossed, he became aware of Spirit Media and extended his kindness by encouraging his friend, Fate, to utilize our services for his marketing needs. Fate wasted no time in reaching out to us and becoming a valued client. Each client we serve is a precious GIFT bestowed by God.

I had the privilege of meeting Frank only once, thanks to Danny, one of my mentors, who arranged a prayer gathering with Frank. During that memorable meeting, we introduced ourselves, engaged in profound discussions about God's kingdom, and joined in prayer. I still have that heartfelt prayer recorded on my phone.

Frank's prayer over me and Spirit Media was bold and audacious, specifically mentioning a building he saw for our company, describing it as "white and huge." It left a profound impact on us. We planned to meet again in two weeks for another prayer session, but the morning we were to meet I received news that Frank had peacefully entered heaven in his sleep. It was a sudden and poignant reminder of how God brought Frank into my life, and just as swiftly, he departed.

Frank left me with an invaluable GIFT—the GIFT of his prayers. Indeed, every person who intercedes for us is a precious GIFT, and prayer itself is a divine GIFT.

When God called me to write this book, He instructed me to compile all the references to His GIFTS in the Bible. Many believers have limited knowledge of God's GIFTS, and only a few live in total dependence on them.

Spirit Media saw its first million in revenue in 2023. In December 2023, God gave us one million dollars in financing. Not only did God miraculously sustain us during 2023, but He positioned us for rapid growth and profitability. I know it's all about "more of Him and more for Him."

In 2024, we moved into the huge white building Frank prayed about. The space is more than adequate for Spirit Media. Not only have God's GIFTS grown and sustained Spirit Media, but the GIFTS of God have multiplied into several companies.

During this year of explosive growth in Spirit Media, God also allowed me to publish two books. Additionally, I traveled on two international mission trips. In October 2023, I returned to India to celebrate twenty-five years of God's faithfulness in the country, visiting four cities and speaking multiple times per day.

Since my first trip to India in 1998, I've now entered India fifty-five times in twenty-five years. Every trip is a GIFT from God. I've taken over 1000 people with me on short-term mission trips. Every traveler is a GIFT from God. We've raised millions of dollars for God's work in India. Every dollar is a GIFT from God.

Hundreds of thousands of Bibles have been distributed in India, each one recognized as a GIFT from God. Surprisingly, over one billion individuals in India have yet to hold a Bible in their hands. Undoubtedly, the GIVER desires for them to have access to His Word! Considering that each Bible costs five dollars, providing them to all would amount to five billion dollars, without even factoring in transportation and logistical expenses.

I'm entirely convinced and convicted that the primary reason the Great Commission remains unfinished is our failure, as God's people, to fully rely on His generous GIFTS.

Perhaps now you grasp the significance of why God has led us to establish Spirit Media and other ventures, completely reliant on His abundant GIFTS.

In Hyderabad, we marked a significant milestone with the publication of *Only God Works* in Hindi, Telugu, and Tamil. This achievement underscores Spirit Media's commitment to translating English books into the world's top twenty spoken languages. Each translation stands as a GIFT from God.

Limitless means limitless.

Earlier, I said, "The world is yet to see what will happen when the people of God, together, all live with the confident expectancy that the Father's going to GIVE it!"

Surely, the time has come for us to change that! Jesus is worthy of us living dependent on the GIFTS of God. God is able to do exceedingly more than we can ask or imagine.

> Now all glory to God, who is able, through his mighty power at work within us, to accomplish infinitely more than we might ask or think. Glory to him in the church and in Christ Jesus through all generations forever and ever! Amen.
> —Ephesians 3:20-21 (NLT)

Merry Christmas!

Sources:

GIFT

Hebrew - MATANA
https://israelforever.org/tzedakah_versus_
matana_the_true_meaning_of_giving/

Greek - dórea
https://biblehub.com/greek/1431.htm

"GIFTS" appears approximately 80 times in the NLT Bible.

GIVE

Hebrew - natan
https://www.kveller.com/jewish-baby-name/
natan/

Greek - Didomi
https://biblehub.com/greek/1325.htm

"GIVE" appears approximately 1073 times in the NLT bible.

GIVES

Hebrew - Natan or Notenn?
https://www.pealim.com/dict/1285-latet/

Greek - dosis/dinei
https://www.wordhippo.com/what-is/the/greek-word-for-d6ba0a23

"GIVES" appears approximately 111 times in the NLT.

GIVEN

Hebrew - natun/Nathiyn
https://www.doitinhebrew.com/Translate/default

Greek - dedoménos
https://www.wordhippo.com/what-is/the/greek-word-for

"GIVEN" appears approximately 754 times in the NLT.

Increasing Your Impact

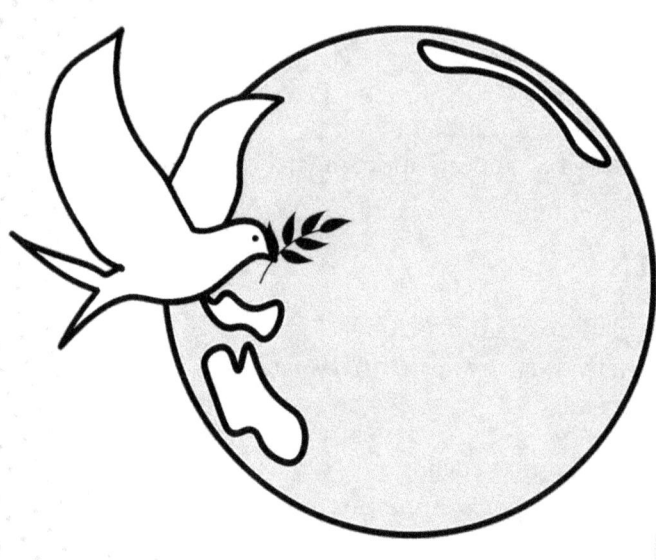

through
Publishing
and Marketing Results

Keeping You In Courage!

KevinWhite.US

Weekly on YouTube @kevinwhiteTV

MORE FROM KEVIN

 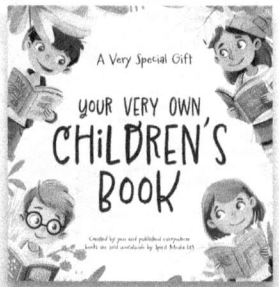 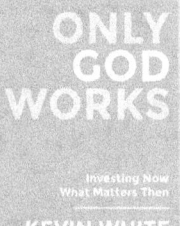